Broken Vows

Broken Vows

Dr. Les Carter

A
JANET
THOMA
BOOK

THOMAS NELSON PUBLISHERS
Nashville

Published in Nashville, Tennessee, by Thomas Nelson, Inc.

Printed in the United States of America.

Scripture quotations are from the NEW KING JAMES
VERSION of the Bible. Copyright © 1979, 1980, 1982,
Thomas Nelson, Inc., Publishers.

Library of Congress Cataloging-in-Publication Data

Carter, Les.
    [Prodigal spouse]
    Broken vows / Les Carter.
        p.   cm.
    "A Janet Thoma book."
    Previously published as: The prodigal spouse. c1990.
    Includes bibliographical references.
    ISBN 0-8407-3349-6
    1. Adultery.   2. Marriage—Religious aspects—Christianity.
I. Title.
[BV4627.A3C37   1991]
248.8'44—dc20   91–22382
                                                  CIP

5 6 7 8 9 10 — 96 95 94

CONTENTS

Acknowledgments

Any project as time-consuming as writing a book is not accomplished without a great deal of support from several sources. The staff of the Minirth-Meier Clinic have been very enthusiastic about this undertaking and have offered much in the way of encouragement and suggestions. Dede Johnston and Beth Deffinbaugh, in particular, have been most helpful in preparing the manuscript and managing my schedule.

Janet Thoma has been a one-of-a-kind editor, and I greatly appreciate her efforts and commitment to this project. She can offer major criticism of my work, and yet I leave smiling after each interchange with her. I don't know how she does it!

Also, I would like to thank my family, Shelba and Cara, for making adjustments so I could have the time to work on this book. An understanding home atmosphere goes a long way toward making my work go smoothly.

Finally, I'd like to express appreciation to the counselees I have worked with through the years, especially those touched by the tragedy of an extramarital affair. By sharing themselves with me, they have helped me gain a clearer understanding of the dynamics of adultery. Each of the illustrations in the pages to follow is derived from actual experiences brought to me in the counseling office. I have taken great care to change the names and the nonessential facts as I relate their stories, but the emotional expressions and the troublesome experiences are very real. I hope you find some help and comfort in these stories.

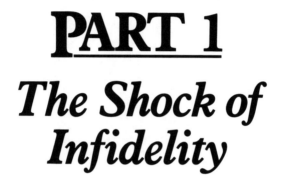

PART 1

The Shock of Infidelity

1

You Are
Not Alone

Sally spoke quite calmly with me regarding her problem. In her late thirties, she could have passed as a woman several years younger. Her short blonde hair was perfectly in place and she wore a designer jogging suit. But despite her pleasant external appearances, she had reason to feel internally wrecked.

"Two weeks ago I found a letter in my husband's briefcase that implicated him in an affair. I wasn't snooping," she explained. "I was looking for last month's bank statement when I saw the letter. It was from a woman who used to work with him. I've met her before but I don't really know her. But I was surprised that Brian showed such poor taste; she's a tramp!"

"Did you confront Brian about the letter?"

"Oh yes. I'm not the kind who can hold things in very well. He tried to make some weak excuse about how it wasn't what I thought. But I finally got him to confess that he had been sleeping with her for about four months."

"Has he said what his plans are for the near future?"

"No, not really. He told me he needed time to think, but I told him I wasn't going to just sit idly by while he plays around. Right now we're at a stalemate."

"Sally, I'm always curious to know about the circumstances that precede an affair. What kind of background do you and Brian have?"

"We really never argued much, at least not until recently. I've always thought that people who had affairs were the real rowdy type. Our home has been fairly calm and stable until now. We've been married almost nineteen years. We may not communicate our feelings to each other, but I always had assumed we would be together forever."

"So to the average observer you would look like the traditional, well-mannered suburban couple."

"I guess so. We both grew up in middle-class families. Both of us went to church every Sunday and did the normal things teenagers do. Brian's dad drank a little too much. I was often frustrated with my mother's hovering, overprotective attitude. But our problems were no worse than anyone else's."

"Would you say that you and Brian had a good send-off in your marriage?"

"Yes, we got married right out of college and were more interested in having fun than anything else. We had a very active social life and went on weekend trips with our friends. We had a lot to keep us busy. But when our boys came along we settled down into a more stable routine—we went back to church and got more involved in the community."

"How old are your boys now?"

"One just turned fourteen and the other is almost twelve. What gets me is that Brian has always been close to our sons and now he seems willing to ruin a good thing for all of us because he's enamored with this woman! I'm convinced he's having his mid-life crisis."

"Looking back, can you see any signs that tension was building?"

She thought about that for a moment. "Well, maybe. We've bickered more than we used to during the last year. Brian has been going to church but not with the enthusiasm he had about ten years ago. I've been a little impatient with the kids, and family disagreements drive Brian crazy."

"So, like you said earlier, the atmosphere has never been extremely violent, but there has been some occasional undercurrent of conflict."

"Yes, you might say that. We never really learned to talk out our problems. Brian likes to withdraw and won't say what's on his mind. I tend to talk too much, which makes him pull further into his shell."

Sally spoke with me in calm, factual tones for more than thirty minutes, but it didn't take much to uncover her delicate emotions. "Sally, I can only imagine how this experience has caused you to feel the whole range of emotions, from deep insecurity to complete rage."

Her look of perfect composure vanished, and her lower lip quivered as she replied in a strained voice, "I wish I could explain how awful I've felt, but it's impossible to express my emotions clearly. I feel I'm a failure as a woman. I feel cheap and dirty. I hate Brian but I still love him. Sometimes when we are sitting quietly in the den I feel a sudden urge to scream at him! But I don't want to lower myself to that level of living. I don't know what to do! I know other good people have probably gone through similar struggles but I feel so all alone. How can I tell my friends that my husband is nothing but a conniving manipulator? I can't say anything to my family because I don't want to spoil our family ties."

"I take it that Brian doesn't want to seek counseling with you."

"Well, maybe he'll come in later. But like I said, he's not the type to talk much about personal matters. This makes me even more angry, because *I'm* the one who's dealing with the problem, not him. He's dropped it in my lap and withdrawn." Sally's mascara was smeared as she looked directly at me and asked, "Am I normal to feel this way?"

Her question illustrated the sense of isolation felt by many rejected spouses. I knew she was hardly alone. Later that day I looked through my appointment schedule for the next week and noticed that a high percentage of my married clients were either currently dealing with this issue or had handled it before. Not all the injured partners were women, as some suppose. In a decade at the Minirth-Meier Clinic I had opened my doors to a wide array of persons trying to make sense of an affair. Some counselees had been well into the throes of divorce proceedings. Others were trying to get out of an affair without the spouse's knowledge. And many, like Sally, were trying to determine how to handle the emotions of disillusionment so an appropriate decision could be made about the family's future.

I conducted some formal research about adultery in the following weeks which revealed that unfaithfulness was more common than I suspected. To allay some of the isolation my counselees feel, I now begin by making it clear: "You are not alone." I often share these statistics to illustrate:

- *Approximately 40 percent of all married men are unfaithful.*

Several major surveys have been conducted to determine the extent of adultery among married men. The results vary according to the populations tested, but it is agreed that about four out of ten men have engaged in sexual relations outside the marriage.[1] This statistic includes brief incidences as well as cases of prolonged affairs. Sally's husband, Brian, was an example of the difficulty many men find in resisting the temporal feel-good experience found with a vulnerable woman.

Sally's jaw dropped when I told her this statistic. "If your percentages are accurate, I probably know several people who have secretly dealt with this problem."

"They're probably just like you in the fact that they wish they could share their burden, but they are hindered because of the embarrassment. Admitting that your husband has found another woman is not the same as telling a friend that you had a disagreement about the children's allowance."

"I wish I could locate some women who have been there. I'd like to know how they handled it. I can assure you that when I'm past all this I'll be more sensitive and less judgmental toward others in the same boat."

"Sally, I'm hoping that you can reduce your deep sense of shame just knowing that you can overcome this problem. While you won't relish hearing others' similar woes, at least you won't feel like some strange misfit."

It is somewhat assuring to know that more men are faithful to their wives than not, but it is troubling to think that such a high percentage of husbands have chosen to seek sexual satisfaction outside of marriage. The reasons for adultery vary. Some men claim to have unsatisfactory marital and/or sexual relations at home, thus "permitting" them to pursue relational needs elsewhere. They feel they deserve better.

I have often heard men complain, as Sally's husband did in a later session, about a lack of support and encouragement, which caused a buildup of anger and emotional tensions. Others say they are in love with their wives but have found another woman who also excites them and is thus deserving of their love. One man explained that he was like a flame that lit two candles—like a flame which has no less fire to give after it

15

lights one candle, he felt he could have a second woman without depleting his ability to love the first. Another rationalization men mention is, "Boys will be boys." They grin sheepishly, admitting that they probably shouldn't "fool around," but they explain they are just playing and having a good time—the act shouldn't be taken seriously.

However men might excuse this conduct, they've crossed the boundary of loyalty and trustworthiness in their marriage. In many cases, men feel guilty and remorseful and try to make amends. Others excuse their infidelity with one of the previous reasons and never evaluate how they might have failed. These men are the most likely to repeat the problem. Brian could easily fall into this category.

- *Fifteen percent of married men report having a series of adulteries.*

Respected sociologist Laurel Richardson, who determined that 40–50 percent of married American males have affairs, also concluded that about a third of those men, roughly 15 percent of the married population, were involved in a series of adulterous relationships.[2] These men are not struggling with a temporary problem. Their behavior is habitual. Such repetitive episodes indicate an addictive need for sex.

"Les, I don't think Brian has a string of women in his past. Maybe I'm naive, but I'm pretty sure this is the only time."

"What signs could make you think otherwise?"

"I'll give you an example. I have a girlfriend whose husband isn't available to her. He's Mr. Self-Important and he's always got an excuse to be gone from home. He seems to have a need for the prima donna treatment and seems attracted to people who build his ego."

"We probably should not stereotype and say all men with this chronic problem are so insensitive, but I think you're accurate to say that they have some very strong ego needs."

"At least Brian is a gentleman. He helps with the children more than most men. I think that stands for something."

Adulterers can often cite a long history of disregard for authority or accountability. Virtues such as kindness and gentleness are tools of manipulation rather than genuine character traits. They take pride in their sexual conquests. When caught by their wives, these men may feel guilt, but it is superficial and thus short-lived.

Frequently, serial adulterers perceive women as objects of pleasure. The "love 'em and leave 'em" attitude protects their emotions and keeps them from getting too emotionally committed. In a few cases such men admit to having such deep feelings of loneliness that they *must* have maximum sexual stimulation, but this tends to be the exception rather than the rule. Most are too macho to admit that the sexual episodes are anything more than masculine fun. This attitude inhibits corrective change.

Most of these men live with little understanding or insight about their real motives. One man told me: "Who knows why I do it? Maybe I just have stronger hormones than other guys. I don't know. But you can be sure I'm not going to give up a normal function."

- *As a man's income increases so does the possibility for adultery.*

Laurel Richardson also reported that men who earned in excess of $60,000 (as of 1985) had a 70 percent possibility of committing adultery.[3] This finding was corroborated by a 1986 finding that cited a 70 percent incidence of adultery for men earning in excess of $70,000.[4] Sally's husband was a likely candidate since he earned more than $70,000. This statistic is consistent with Jesus' warning, "It is easier for a camel to go through the eye of a needle than for a rich man to enter the kingdom of God" (Matt. 19:24).

Three major factors lie behind this relationship between prosperity and adultery: power, the habit of acquisition, and a "reward mentality." The first is related to power.

POWER

Most men who command a high salary, like Brian, are either in charge of a contingent of people or are sole proprietors of businesses and are accustomed to having their way.

For example, Brian had climbed steadily within his company. He began his career as a computer analyst and worked himself into a supervisory position over eighty people. He set his sights on reaching the top and would not be stopped.

In the process of accumulating power, men not only become accustomed to favored treatment, they grow to expect it. They develop an attitude that causes them to assume others should do as they say simply because they say it. As the experience of power grows so does the assumption of privilege. A feeling of "you can't deny me" spreads beyond the world of work and into personal life. If problems or dissatisfactions arise at home this mind-set becomes more evident. It has been said that power corrupts. This can be true in the powerful person's morality.

A HABIT OF ACQUISITION

When people have wealth and affluence they surround themselves with material objects. Houses, cars, or clothes become more than just functional—they become statements of success. Some materialistic cynics have said: "He who dies with the most toys wins." The desire to acquire spills over into the realm of relationships. Privileged people may assume that if a sexual relationship within marriage goes sour, they should be free to find another to replace it. Brian had broadened this "replace my rusty toy" philosophy to include the slightest crack in his relationship with his wife.

A REWARD MENTALITY

Most men do not begin their careers with large salaries. They spend years working long hours to achieve status, perhaps to the detriment of personal relations or with little family involvement. Once they reach a satisfactory financial plateau, they may nurse ideas of self-gratification. They are ready to take a break from ladder-climbing to enjoy themselves. Sexuality offers a quick feel-good sensation, so adultery is a common choice.

Sally put her finger on this when she told me, "The last few years Brian has been talking more selfishly about what the company owed him. He kept saying that he had put in long hours and ignored vacation days because he was so committed to company growth."

"Let me guess . . . he's been talking about wanting more time to pursue the fun things in life."

"You got it. He's been more interested in sports and leisure activities. In some ways this has been good because he's spent time having fun with the boys. But all along I've had the uncomfortable feeling that he was too willing to escape responsibilities."

"It seems that part of the motivation for the affair may have been to enjoy some of the gusto he missed because of his career building. It will help you understand this when you're trying to fit the pieces together, explaining the whys of it all."

• *About one-third of all married women have had an extramarital affair.*

Earlier I mentioned that women were the unfaithful spouses in some of my counseling cases. Several studies and surveys have tried to determine the extent of adultery among married women. Yet the most respected surveys vary widely in their findings. This is due to the different populations tested. According to *Time* magazine the percentages of married women involved in affairs ranged from 21 to 43 percent.[5] A more recent report narrowed the percentage to 30 to 36 percent.[6]

Most women involved in extramarital affairs cite loneliness in the current marriage, which creates a yearning to be accepted and loved, as the reason for their affair. Men may also report this as a factor in infidelity, but women seem especially vulnerable to temptations when emotional needs are unfulfilled. Women are not always the aggressors in these affairs, although they can deliberately send signals of availability to potential suitors. Interestingly, Sally admitted that she felt tempted to explore sexual relationships in retaliation to her husband's affair. By admitting her own vulnerability, Sally was more willing to understand Brian's struggles.

The most vulnerable time for a woman to have an affair is between ages thirty-five and thirty-nine,[7] according to researcher, R. J. Levin. By the time a woman reaches her late thirties, her children are becoming less dependent. Women in this age range may try to hold on to every bit of youth possible, causing a type of pre-mid-life crisis. Additionally, her husband may be at the peak of status-seeking in his career, and she may be even more vulnerable because she feels isolated from him.

"Sally, I can tell that Brian's affair has caused you to consider your own weaknesses. What thoughts have you had about sexual temptations?"

She paused, then answered, "I've found that as Brian and I move into the middle-aged years, things in our marriage aren't as settled as I assumed they would be. We have more money than we ever had before, but now I look back at our mid-twenties and think that we didn't have it so bad, even though we were just making it from paycheck to paycheck."

"What's different between now and then?"

"Well, Brian spends the same hours away from home as he always did, but now I miss him more. I thought that at some point in his career he would get more involved in my world. But it's not happening."

"And that makes your loneliness all the more intense."

"It sure does. Then I compare Brian to other men his age and wonder why he can't be more of a husband. I admit I've had my own fantasies about finding a new Mr. Right. My life hasn't unfolded as I thought it should."

"You're fortunate you haven't been caught in too vulnerable a situation. You might be dealing with the same problem as Brian. I appreciate your candid self-evaluation."

- *There is a lack of eligible bachelors for single women over age 25.*

Many women grow up with the idea that "The right man is out there, I just have to find him." That's no longer so. The 1980 census showed that there were not enough men to marry every woman in the United States: There are 21.5 million unmarried men to just under 30 million unmarried women. One researcher determined that there were 39 percent more unmarried women than men under the age of thirty; 42 percent more unmarried women than men in the thirty to forty-four age range; and 56 percent more women than men in the forty-five to sixty-four age range.[8]

Many single women are content with their lifestyle, but some fear that they will never be able to share a man's love. As a result, some actually pursue men, whether they are married or not, to fulfill their sexual desires.

One thirty-six-year-old woman told me unapologetically, "I'm not getting any younger, so I have to take what I can get. When Mike and I began seeing each other, I knew he was married. I decided if his wife wanted to hold him, she would have to treat him better than I could. All's fair in love and war!" Many women live with the idea that settling for second best is better than having nothing at all.

The majority of these single women are in the work force where they get to know their male counterparts well. Office romances build over time due to repeated exposures to each other and a similarity of interests. The wives of these men often spend less time with their husbands than the women who work with them do. Sally understood better the temptations her husband faced when she saw a clearer picture of the world he lived in each day.

- *Premarital promiscuity is on the rise.*

"Les, I don't know the statistics, but I'm certain today's social atmosphere is more permissive than when I grew up," Sally offered. "Temptations are much greater now for kids to be promiscuous, and I can't help but think that this has an effect on the adult world." I agree. There is indeed a high level of promiscuity among the young which has an influence on adult behavior. Ideally, adults should be setting the standards for the young, but this is not always the case. Envious of or attracted to adolescent sexual freedoms, many adults adopt the loose standards practiced by their younger counterparts.

In their incisive book, *Why Wait?,* Josh McDowell and Dick Day examine the trends in promiscuity among American adolescents. Whereas "saving" oneself for marriage was once held in high regard, in the 1980s 81 percent of the males and 67 percent of the females engaged in premarital sex before age twenty.[9] This staggering statistic does not directly relate to matters of adultery, but it is a powerful index of our permissive sexual milieu. America's youth reflect the overall social climate.

Why is premarital promiscuity so common? This question has many and varied answers. Sex is publicly displayed in more blatant and seductive ways than ever before. Television programs and movies communicate an obvious disregard for traditional family values. They depict as "normal" such alternatives as homosexuality, live-in arrangements, and casual promiscuity. Men and women who are desperate to go to bed with any available partner are portrayed as humorous and lovable. Monogamous relationships confined to marriage are considered too old-fashioned to be taken seriously. To be "with it," you should endorse unbridled sexual expression.

The responsibility for increased promiscuity cannot be solely accorded to the entertainment industry. Other factors are also involved. The many touch-of-the-finger conveniences engender an impatience which inhibits our willingness to take time in relational maturation. We want what we want *now.* With more mothers in the work force, many children spend extra hours each week without the special guidance and accountability a hands-on parent provides. In addition, clothing is more provocative. There are more exciting enticements to spend free time in self-indulgent activities. Conservative values and Christian ethics are taboo in many educational settings. These elements and others feed a general moral decay that spills over into matters of sexual behavior. A climate of greater sexual freedoms leads many adults to follow suit in the trends endorsed by the young.

- *Marital dissatisfaction translates into sexual yearning.*

In studying the correlation between marital and sexual satisfaction, researchers have determined that couples who are happy with their marital sexual relations are less likely to leave a marriage.[10] The high correlation between marital dissatisfaction and sexual frustration underscores the need to preserve morality by learning to more effectively handle emotions and improve communication in the home.

Sally told me during one counseling session, "When Brian and I married we felt a genuine love for each other but we were very naive about communication skills. Neither of us was experienced in handling tough emotional issues, so they often got swept under the rug. More than once Brian said he was tired of having to try so hard to keep the communication lines open."

Sexual promiscuity is frequently a direct result of long-standing emotional and communication difficulties. These cannot be resolved without a great deal of personal introspection and interpersonal cooperation. I explained to Sally that, by recognizing her own needs, she could gain many insights to help her reestablish personal satisfaction and marital communication. We outlined several major issues to be addressed in our counseling sessions. First, she needed to define the boundaries for her marriage while it was still in limbo. This would mean exploring some logistical issues so ground rules could be agreed upon: Should they separate? What should the children be told? How much counseling should she insist upon?

I realized that Sally needed permission to express and examine the varied emotions she carried by herself. It would be impossible for her to know how to interact with Brian if she was too absorbed with her internal tensions.

Next, I explained that I wanted her to have an understanding of the reasons motivating Brian's affair. He eventually submitted to counseling and then the two were able to discuss his frustrations. Finally, we planned to examine alternative means of handling emotions and communications in a manner that would improve marital harmony.

The following chapters will look more closely at the problems inherent in an unfaithful situation. The next chapter addresses some of the same "ground rules" questions posed by Sally.

2

Ground Rules for an Interim Relationship

The middle-aged couple calmly sitting in my waiting room would appear to have no more problems than any other couple. The husband, Doug, displayed a look of confidence. He spoke pleasantly with the secretaries and firmly shook my hand, as if he were genuinely pleased to meet me. Helen, his wife, seemed accustomed to living in his shadow. She was more reserved, even withdrawn, in our initial greetings. After exchanging a few informal words, they explained why they had come to me.

Helen and Doug sought counseling because he had confessed to a year-long affair with Shirley. Shortly afterward he had moved into an apartment to sort through his options. During the first session Doug explained how miserable he was by himself and that he wanted quick reconciliation, "Honey, you have to understand that what's done is done. We have to put it behind us and get on with the rest of our lives."

Helen felt insecure with Doug's new commitment to their marriage. "How can I know that you won't go back to Shirley or be attracted by some other woman?" she asked. "You've spent at least a year hiding the truth from me, and I can't fully trust you!"

Doug leaned toward Helen and said, "Look, you're going to have to realize that my problems are finished. I'm tired of staying in my cheap apartment. I want to come back where I belong."

"Doug, I'd like to see us get back together, but you're pushing me. Can't we be more careful in the way we do this?"

When counseling a couple, logistical questions such as living arrangements or accountability procedures must often be discussed first. Usually changes cannot be made in the relationship until logistical issues are settled.

SHOULD WE SEPARATE?

It is natural that Helen and Doug disagree about living arrangements—their perspectives are entirely different. Doug struggled with his problem of infidelity for a year and was eager to put the ordeal to rest. However, Helen had known about it for only a few days and her emotions were still unsettled.

In many cases, separation may be the only route to true healing since an affair involves a strong outside attachment. But separate living arrangements should be carefully considered since it has risks. Doug and Helen had separated before they came in for counseling, but Doug felt that he made the move too hastily. He felt that separation would hinder the healing process. Helen felt it might force them both to take time for some real soul-searching.

Separation becomes a very viable choice in cases involving a long-standing affair (those lasting several weeks or more). In these situations the attachment to the third person is usually strong and will take time to dissolve. Separation is also very common in cases involving multiple brief affairs. The unfaithful spouse must see a clear signal that a three-way relationship will not be tolerated. This is particularly true when the affair is not yet over. I have witnessed many situations where the adulterer took the injured mate's leniency as a license to continue illicit behavior. When no consequences are forthcoming, self-indulgence can run rampant.

Helen and Doug could not deal with the housing issue until Doug's question "What do I have to do to regain your trust?" was answered. I asked Helen, "What could Doug do to show you he can be trusted to reestablish residence with you?"

Helen had thought about this frequently and was quite specific in her requests.

"First, I have to know that he has said good-bye to Shirley. After all, he's apparently been seeing her for at least a year. I'm tired of all his unexplained time away from home. Second, I want Doug to be fully open about his finances so he can't hide the money he spends on her. Third, I want him to prove to me that he is really capable of being a true partner. That includes no sex for now. I want him to see me as a friend, rather than just his plaything. This means we'll spend time talking and becoming reacquainted with each other's needs. Also, I'd like to see some genuine interest in his spiritual growth. When he shows consistency in these areas, I'll know he is ready to be the husband I need."

"Doug, that's a pretty tall order. What do you think?"

A chagrined look crossed Doug's face. "It doesn't look like I have much choice. I really mean it when I say that I want her to be my wife. I'll do what it takes to prove it."

Together the three of us set some guidelines to gradually direct their relationship back toward a full marital union. At Helen's request they decided to remain separated the first few weeks—enjoying several hours together on the weekends.

Since the goal was to establish a friendship pattern there would be no sexual contact. On weekdays they would maintain some phone contact, interspersed with brief visits. Doug was to let Helen know of his whereabouts even when she did not ask. He was reluctant to disclose his finances but agreed to do so as a gesture of openness. They set up an operating budget to cover the financial needs for two households.

Some fearful spouses protest the idea of separation, claiming that the mate might be pushed further into the lover's arms. Therefore, they hold on for dear life, thinking they have more security by keeping a close eye on their unfaithful spouse.

My experience indicates that if one spouse needs to desperately cling to the other to keep the marriage alive, the relationship is very unstable. Insecurity, rather than free choice controls the couple's relationship. It is better to give the spouse freedom to choose his or her commitment.

This is not to say that *every* long-term extramarital affair should result in separation of the spouses. In some cases, the shame of the exposed affair is so powerful and the desire for repentance so real that the couple would do best to capitalize on this. Sometimes the unfaithful spouse is actually relieved to be caught and is immediately ready to start a new way of life. The faithful spouse quickly may be able to muster the trust necessary to move forward.

In cases involving a brief affair or a one-time escapade, the need for separation diminishes. The purpose of any separation is to allow time for the faithful spouse to deal with his or her emotions and the unfaithful spouse to register genuine repentance. If the mate had a very brief affair, but cannot recommit to a lasting relationship, a separation may be helpful. If, on the other hand, there is true repentance and a willingness to remedy the wrong, a separation could be ill-advised.

HOW LONG SHOULD A SEPARATION LAST?

When an affair has been brief, the spouse may have been releasing pent-up anger, rather than expressing an emotional commitment to a third party. In those situations a briefer separation time may be appropriate, provided that both spouses are willing to explore ways to create a better home environment.

The guidelines that Helen and Doug set stabilized the tension between them and added a comfortable predictability to their relationship. This allowed them to concentrate on the problems between them during our weekly counseling sessions.

After a month of living by these guidelines, Helen agreed to Doug's staying overnight on weekends without sexual contact. Doug exercised discipline, and after about six weeks, Helen took a weekend trip with him as a "second honeymoon." Soon after, Doug moved back home.

Doug and Helen admitted that they did not like their separation but it was good for them. Doug expressed it well: "I needed the time to get away and think about where my life was headed. And I know Helen used her time in a similar way. The time apart was a real jolt to our system, but that's not all bad since it's obvious our system needed shaking up."

A separation might last a month or two, with the unfaithful spouse staying in a short-term location, as Doug did. But when the unfaithful spouse is uncertain about a continuing commitment to the marriage, a longer separation time may be essential. Any indication of a continuing interest in the third party should be viewed as a sign that more time is needed to make major attitudinal changes. This time should not be accompanied by all the comforts of home. If the adulterer is allowed to have it both ways, that is precisely what will happen. It is unfair for the injured mate to negotiate with the spouse, knowing the third person is waiting in case temporary troubles result during reconciliation.

When the other party is out of the way, the couple can determine the length of separation based on their growing level of comfort with one another. Dates for the purpose of light fun should be set, as should conferences for the sake of sharing feelings and goals. As the level of optimism increases, so should the amount of contact. I have known couples to move back into full living arrangements in just a few weeks, and I have known some to take several months. The time limit should be flexible. A pastor or professional counselor may assist in determining this.

Doug and Helen had demonstrated a willingness to maturely examine the factors leading to his affair, so their separation was relatively brief (ten weeks), given the length of the affair. It is not unusual for a separation to last up to more than six months. If it stretches beyond a year this is generally a sign of passive aggressiveness and an unwillingness to live in mutual submission.

SHOULD I CONFRONT THE THIRD PARTY?

The injured mate will likely express tremendous curiosity about the one involved with the spouse. This is particularly true when the other person is a mysterious unknown entity. The injured spouse can't help wondering, "Is so-and-so more alluring?" "Sexier?" "More fun to be with?" "More intelligent?" Knowing about the other person helps the injured party come to terms with what happened. Such curiosity is very normal. Few people like an unresolved mystery.

In a private conversation, Helen told me that through some detective work she had learned the identity of Doug's former mistress. Then she had parked outside this woman's apartment one Saturday just to get a glimpse of her.

"I expected to find a gorgeous model who would turn every man's head, but instead she reminded me of one of my close friends. She was somewhat plain looking, and she really didn't have the sultry appearance I anticipated. I'm not sure if I was disappointed or not, but at least I was satisfied in knowing who she was and where she lived." Helen chose not to ask Doug any intimate questions because she knew he would never divulge the answers, and besides, she wisely knew that such information could only become grounds for haunting mental images.

The adulterer should be willing to give general facts about the other person and the circumstances surrounding the affair. The confession should not necessarily include minute details that would only increase the injured spouse's emotional trauma or burden the couple's efforts to restore their marriage. I do not encourage further deception after the affair is exposed, but I believe tact is needed. Sordid details of sexual activity and covert behaviors may overload the injured mate emotionally. Generally, the third person's identity and whereabouts should be shared so the spouse knows that the secrecy is broken. And enough should be shared about the extent of the involvement so remorse can be properly registered. The person who wants to know every name, date, and person who saw them together is acting in paranoia and is craving excessive control.

For example, one husband repeatedly demanded that his wife tell him her boyfriend's name and address. He insisted on knowing every single date that they met. And he wanted the name of every acquaintance who had seen them in public. When I talked with this man it was clear that he was an extremely dominating man who would not act rationally if he had the information he was demanding. I told his wife that under more rational circumstances knowing some of the details would probably help her mate emotionally, but his irrationality was a signal to remain general in her disclosures.

Only under very special circumstances should an actual confrontation with the third party occur. First, if there is substantial evidence that the affair might continue it may be beneficial for the third party to see the spouse who is being "swindled." A face-to-face confrontation may take away some of the thrill of secrecy. Second, if the third person will be in the couple's social circle in the future, as in the case of a coworking situation, it can be productive for the injured mate to convey concern about any continuing contact with the spouse. Finally, if the other party is gossiping about the affair with the intent of hurting the jilted spouse, a confrontation may prove necessary to communicate self-respect. For instance, one injured wife spoke to her husband's former liaison telling her of the reconciliation and that her brazenness was not going to hamper their determination to press forward. After the discussion the mistress completely withdrew from the husband's social surroundings.

If there is a desire to take vengeance or a morbid curiosity, personal contact with the third party would prove detrimental to the marriage and ultimately to the injured mate's dignity.

WHAT SHOULD WE TELL THE CHILDREN?

Not all adultery situations become known to the children; if this is the case, it is usually best to leave it that way. It is true that children should learn to manage real-life problems, but it is best to refrain from making them feel caught in the middle of the parents' problems. Children who learn about a major strain between Mom and Dad will likely be torn regarding which side to team with. They often have difficulty being objective in sorting through the reasons why the affair occurred. This is especially true when the children are in their early teens or younger.

However, sometimes children sense a tremendous tension between their parents, prompting them to ask very pointed questions. Today's kids are not completely naive about sexual matters and are quite capable of fitting pieces of the puzzle together, drawing some accurate conclusions. Some children are told the facts by others. Adult children are capable of sorting out suspicion and innuendos and will usually surmise the problem. In these situations, straight talk is usually required, though references to sexual details should be minimized.

The ultimate goal in sharing facts with the child is to be honest, without deliberately attempting to undermine the child's feelings for either parent. It is preferable for the erring parent to explain the situation in person. If that is impossible, the remaining parent should tell the facts without insinuating judgment. Feelings of hurt and confusion are fair topics of discussion, as is the uncertainty about the future. Efforts to elicit the child's thoughts should be made, but not forcibly.

One of the major issues Doug and Helen confronted was to decide what to say to their sixteen-year-old daughter and ten-year-old son. Since Doug had been out of the house for several weeks the children already knew there were problems. Doug had already told each of them that he was unhappy and needed to get away to relieve feelings of stress.

Before Doug talked directly to the children, I cautioned him, "It would be best to refrain from stating that you were trying to decide if you still loved their mother."

"But why shouldn't I say that, since it sums up part of my dilemma?"

"Kids will interpret your words from a very self-oriented point of view. If you tell them that you might not love Mom, their thoughts will be 'If he can't love Mom, he probably won't love me.'"

35

"So how can I best approach it?"

"Just speak personally to them about some of the confusion in your emotions and priorities. Let them know that you have let too much time go by without resolving frustrations, and let them understand that you had to take time out to let God give you clear direction about the best way to handle your family responsibilities."

Doug had a private talk with each of his children. Without going into details about the affair, he shared very personally that he had to reevaluate his spiritual goals and the family commitments he made years ago. He assured them that he was going to remain married to their mother and that he would be more sensitive to their needs. He gave each of them a chance to share their feelings, although they did not have much to say at the time. A week or so later, they each inquired about divorce, and Doug had a chance to discuss their emotions more specifically, reassuring them that he would stay.

"Les, it felt strange to talk with my kids on such a vulnerable level. But it was good for me, and I sense that we can have a new attitude of openness in our home. My daughter especially needed to hear me say 'I love you,' and she has talked with me about feeling afraid that her mother would have to get a job and support the family. That opened the door for some good interaction."

It is usually enough for younger children to learn that Mom and Dad are having to take time out to handle some problems in their marriage. (This changes if the adulterous spouse determines to leave the marriage for that other person.) A child entering the teen years becomes more worldly-wise and direct communication may be warranted, focusing on the emotions and confusion related to personal struggles. It must be emphasized that the injured spouse is helping no one by slandering the unfaithful mate before the children. Once the child is given the facts, the child should have time to sort through his or her emotions without also being burdened by the parents' interpersonal tensions.

DO WE *HAVE TO* STAY MARRIED?

Virtually every case of adultery leads to questions about the future viability of the marriage. Once the line of sexual fidelity is crossed, it will require great effort to maintain accountability and reestablish trust. Many couples decide that the effort is either futile or too difficult, so they opt for divorce. Citing Matthew 19:9 or 1 Corinthians 7:15, they determine that they are well within their scriptural rights to do so:

> Whoever divorces his wife, *except for sexual immorality,* and marries another, commits adultery (italics added).

> If the unbeliever departs, let him depart; a brother or sister is not under bondage in such cases.

Others, determined to let God's grace live through them, choose to stay married. Actually, either option is open, and it is up to the individuals involved to determine God's guidance in their lives.

The key is to dismiss any legalistic notion of what is supposed to or not supposed to occur. The New Testament instructions regarding divorce were never meant to be applied in a legalistic manner. The statements are definitive and should be taken seriously but are not to be implemented with such rigidness that God's will is not considered.

When adultery occurs a couple does not *have to* stay married. They are free to divorce, and the injured party has the full assurance of God's guidance (so does the adulterer when there is genuine repentance). The better question is: Which choice will be more advantageous for spiritual growth? In some cases, individuals are so damaged by adultery that the best choice is to make a clean break in order to rebuild spiritually. In other cases the pain is great, but it would only become worse by a divorce. For example, when a divorce is pursued even when reconciliation efforts might have been viable, resentments and self-doubt may plague the spouses much longer than the scars of an affair. It is always best to seek resolutions which show a commitment to letting God be in control of the marriage.

IS COUNSELING ALWAYS NECESSARY?

As a psychotherapist I have a strong bias toward the usefulness of counseling with the problem of infidelity. A major dynamic common to this behavior is deception, beginning with the deception of self. Restoration requires stark honesty, and it may be difficult for the once deceptive person to be open to incisive self-analysis. Furthermore, the injured spouse can have great confusion regarding the best course to take. Christian counseling may prove helpful by objectively ferreting out strategies for personal growth.

To receive counseling requires humility—it implies a type of neediness or uncertainty. For this reason many people resist counseling. I do not encourage one spouse to coerce a reluctant spouse into treatment; successful counseling is contingent upon the willingness to be helped. When a person enters counseling with a sour attitude, it may be counterproductive. It can set off a power struggle within the marriage and inhibit the chances for counseling at a later date.

However, when counseling is refused, the chances of restoration diminish. Such unwillingness usually indicates a continuing false pride and a preference to deny or overlook serious personal adjustments needing repair.

If a spouse needs counseling but refuses it, the remaining

partner has two primary options: (1) the willing spouse can seek counseling regarding ways to handle the situation; (2) accountability measures may be applied to persuade the resistant partner to develop a personal growth pattern, inhibiting future episodes of marital discord. Specifically, this means a continuation of full marital norms only if activities are fully disclosed. It should be understood that any continuation of adulterous activity will result in separation or divorce proceedings.

Doug and Helen found great relief in knowing that they could agree on the logistical problems caused by his unfaithfulness. Feeling as if they now had a "game plan," they were free to concentrate on the more complex emotional issues that must be resolved. Helen struggled with the grief related to the loss of her marriage's innocence; Doug knew that he needed to comprehend the emotional reasons for his behavior. We continued our sessions with the intent of bringing closure to these matters.

In the chapters to follow we will examine the emotional fallout related to a discovered affair.

3

Your Emotions: A Natural Part of Grieving

Ron was an electrician. His rough hands and weathered face indicated that he was no stranger to hard work and manly qualities. He was not the type to wear the title "emotional weakling." His wife had been acting unusually distant during the last couple of months, and he was at his wit's end trying to make sense of his feelings.

"My whole world seems to be crumbling. Laura and I have not had a perfect relationship but we got along okay. We've had arguments but no more than any other couple. But I don't know what to think now that she is going through this crisis with the other man! Sometimes I feel very bitter and other times I just shake my head in bewilderment. There are moments when I think I never want to see her again, yet I still love her. I've *never* felt this unsettled."

Ron expressed the normal sentiments of an injured mate who has recently learned of a spouse's infidelity. Many spouses may suspect their mate is involved in an affair, but no one is fully prepared for the emotions that follow its revelation. For a while life is put on hold as the injured spouse considers life-changing decisions. Should I remain married? How will I handle this with my parents? How can I go out in public without looking as if I've just been to a funeral?

Ron told me that his wife, Laura, had been seeing a man she knew prior to their marriage. She and David became re-acquainted after fifteen years when they met at their children's soccer games. In the following weeks Laura suggested that the two families get together for social outings and Ron agreed. At first Ron had no reason to feel jealous, but he began to suspect that David and Laura were getting too friendly. Ron subtly suggested that Laura might be flirting with David, but she brushed it off so whimsically that he felt foolish for even thinking it.

After Ron noticed several unexplained absences from Laura's normal routine, he asked her if she was sexually involved with David. Laura began to cry and never answered Ron directly. A few days later one of Laura's friends told Ron that his suspicions were true. Ron again asked Laura about David, but she would not answer his pointed questions. She merely stonewalled him.

"Les, I'm not normally an uptight person but right now I'm torn up. I have a chance to move to a new city with a large contractor, which would mean a nice pay raise. But I have no desire to make any changes if there's a good chance that my wife won't go with me. I'm depressed almost all the time. I can't concentrate. I'm not friendly anymore. My co-workers and friends see that something is wrong, and when anyone asks I just tell them I'm under stress."

"Your emotions are made more volatile by Laura's evasion," I told Ron. "You have no way of tying up loose ends with her."

"That's right. She knows that I know the truth and that it's torturing me, but she doesn't seem to care. If I wasn't a civilized man, there's no telling what I'd say or do. I'm thinking about letting her go completely."

"That's a bridge that must be crossed soon," I admitted. "But in the meantime we need to keep your emotions under control."

When an affair is discovered, the offended spouse is likely to experience grief that could last several months or longer. Grief is multifaceted. It is the emotion of loss and includes struggles with feelings of sadness, hurt, anger, confusion, guilt, depression, and loneliness. Grieving individuals try to make sense of a great disappointment, yet vary widely in their emotional expressions.

For example, two women compared notes regarding the discovery of their husbands' affairs. One expressed anger, bordering on rage, that her husband would be so "low down" as to degrade himself in such a forbidden relationship. She railed against his lack of gratitude for the many chores she did for him daily and for her constant availability whenever he expressed a need. She had been played for a fool, and she was determined to let him know that he was going to be "taken to the cleaners" in a nasty divorce suit.

The other woman was much more reserved in her reaction. She expressed great shame because she had not foreseen the affair. She felt extremely lonely because she did not know how to express herself to her husband, and she was afraid of the possibility of becoming a divorcee.

Was either of these women in error in her response to the affair? Not necessarily. They each felt a great loss in very different ways.

IDENTIFYING THE ELEMENTS OF GRIEF

When I counseled Ron, I told him that before his emotions could become settled, he first needed to openly identify them. I do not encourage cathartic screaming, but told him, "You do not need to play hero by pretending that all is well when it isn't."

I suggested that he write out his emotions, perhaps in the form of an unmailed letter to Laura or the other man. This would release his obsessive thoughts. I also asked him to share freely with me each time we met. I knew that he was experiencing grief over the loss of his marriage's innocence. I wanted him to have the chance to let his emotions be heard. He found our sessions helpful since I was the only one who would let him express fears or inadequacies without immediately trying to give him answers.

The injured spouse must allow grief to run its course. Feelings should be allowed the full range of exploration. As these are identified and expressed, the injured mate will discover that the emotions of grief are broad.

Shock

For many the immediate response to an affair is shock and disbelief. An affair represents a behavior outside the boundaries of normalcy; almost no one enters marriage with the forethought of such an intrusion. Most couples have some expectation of making their marriage relationship distinct from all other relationships. When a mate learns that their exclusive sexual union is no longer unique, it is only natural to have this emotion. In fact, a lack of shock might indicate a cavalier attitude toward the sanctity of marriage.

When shock occurs, an emotional numbness may temporarily exist as attempts are made to correlate the newly revealed facts. A type of denial may emerge. The injured spouse, like Ron, may have such thoughts as:

- "I just can't believe this is happening."
- "I was afraid of something like this but now it seems too strange to be true."

- "I've got to have some time to myself so I can come to grips with this."
- "I feel so foolish because I didn't see it coming."

In a sense the shock reaction serves as an emotional transition between a period of presumed normalcy and a period of turbulence. During this time there is usually a flood of thoughts, often obsessive in nature, regarding the different courses of action that might be followed. For example, the injured mate might mentally retrace recent events that hinted at the presence of an affair. A grand speech may be rehearsed over and over, telling the spouse exactly how unfair this wound is. Confusion is almost invariably experienced because of the ever-changing nature of these obsessions. Such confusion is normal. It alerts the individual to the need to patiently sift through options since they are not likely to be easily and quickly deciphered.

The danger to avoid is extreme shock—clinging to such a powerful sense of denial (*can this really be happening to* me?) that the reaction is subtle pride. *Other people have this problem, but surely* my *marriage is immune from such struggles.* This promotes a "how dare this happen" arrogance. Extreme shock may also create an unhealthy feeling of martyrdom, which can inhibit personal restoration. In both cases, the preoccupation with personal feelings and disappointment leads to losing touch with logic.

Anger

Occasionally injured mates state that they feel no anger toward the adulterer. Not only is this abnormal, it is *not* healthy. No person should enjoy the prospect of living in anger, but neither should a person be so intent on being the perfect picture of calm that allows no emotion. Some issues deserve angry responses, and adultery is one of them. To sidestep anger a person must be void of deep convictions.

However, the purpose of anger should never be punitive. Vengeance belongs to God alone. In the case of adultery, the purpose of the injured spouse's anger is (1) to communicate a need for personal respect and (2) to stand firmly for godly convictions. Jesus Himself expressed anger when exposed to people who presumed themselves to be above the laws of God or who demonstrated blatant disregard for the worth of a fellow human. In communicating anger, He publicly aligned Himself to the Father, hoping to make others measure themselves against the standard of righteousness. An injured mate can feel right about expressing anger as long as it is within the context of constructively communicating right convictions.

Ron clenched his fists as he shared his struggle to maintain balanced anger upon learning of Laura's affair. "My first reaction was to find the other man so I could tell him off, then beat the living daylights out of him. Next I wanted to give my wife a tongue-lashing that she would never forget. I was so mad that I was an explosion waiting to happen."

"This whole affair has brought out a side of your personality that is not often displayed," I said. Ron had told me enough about himself that I knew how reserved he was. "Ron, you must have experienced deep emotions."

"I sure have, but I had to quickly ask myself about the validity of my feelings. I concluded that I was right to be angry because it indicated that I stood for something. But I also decided that if I went overboard with my emotions I would be responding to sin with sin, and that would make me a hypocrite."

"Ron, you are maintaining balance. It's good that you are being honest about your anger, yet you are being careful not to let it overwhelm you. In the long run this will keep you from chronic feelings of defeat."

Ephesians 4:26 tells us to be angry without sin. This means that hurt and disappointment can be expressed, but without condemnation. In the case of Ron and Laura, Ron decided that he would express his anger by firmly drawing his lines of concern.

"Laura, I know that you are not admitting what happened, and I have decided not to persistently harp on the issue. But I want you to know that I cannot in good conscience accept any further contact with David. I'm hurt and confused, but I'm going to allow several weeks to pass to get a feel for the decision we should make. In the meantime I hope we can make some effort to reestablish our ties with each other."

Self-preserving boundaries can be laid without inflicting misery. Convictions can be firmly declared without a dictatorial spirit. Ephesians 4:27 indicates that the person who chooses to let sin infiltrate anger will be playing into the hands of Satan. Whereas a lack of anger implies a lack of conviction, an excess of anger implies deep insecurity masked by a need for control.

Guilt

Injured mates can always accuse the adulterer of wrongdoing, but these persons are usually not without some question regarding their own guilt. Some find this emotion to be minor, others experience it in abundance. A nagging question may plague the injured spouse: "Could I have done anything to prevent this from happening?" These persons are either painfully aware that they did not provide a wholesome atmosphere for marital growth, or they feel inadequate—they did not possess the necessary qualities to keep the mate around.

There can be a healthy aspect to guilt if it promotes constructive self-examination, which leads directly to personal improvements. The injured mate should not accept major responsibility for a spouse's unfaithfulness, but it is good to consider the possibility that one's mannerisms did not help the marital union. In some cases injured spouses conclude that they did not contribute to the affair, but that it was an independent act of rebellion on the part of the mate. Their experiences with guilt will be brief.

In other instances honesty leads to the conclusion that the injured mate actually helped push the adulterer out. The emotion prompts painful self-examination about attitudes and behaviors in need of change. If the struggles with guilt lead to the identification of some wrongdoing by the injured mate, it serves the function of producing a repentant spirit and restorative ways.

At first, Ron wanted Laura to take full responsibility for her actions. I had no desire to make Ron feel responsible for her decisions, but I urged him to examine how he might make some adjustments which would diminish the possibility for a repeat. He admitted that he was often perfectionistic and ignored Laura's requests for a more relaxed spirit. He recognized that he was often too willing to let their communication sit on the back burner for weeks, leaving her frustrated and lonely. Ron learned that part of the healing process would include some restructuring of his sensitivities. He also saw that his initial unwillingness to admit guilt was merely a defense for his feelings of insecurity which had been unexpectedly exposed.

As with anger, it is best to approach guilt in a "middle of the road" style. It is healthy to take an honest inventory of one's pluses and minuses if it does not lead to self-degradation. Ron once told me, "In my lowest moments I have thought that if I had been married to someone like me, I might cheat too." We quickly agreed that he was being too hard on himself. Excessive guilt usually accompanies an unrealistic assumption that one should always be the perfect spouse.

Loneliness

God calls us to be joined together in harmonious relations for the purpose of sharing His love. He wants us to have strong bonds of loyalty in our relationships. He wants us to draw strength from a joint commitment to His purposes, knowing that such oneness enhances joy and peace. Philippians 2:2 says: "Fulfill my joy by being like-minded, having the same love, being of one accord, of one mind." This thought is especially applicable to marriage. Upon creating Adam, God stated that it was not good that he be alone, so God created the marital union to provide psychological completion.

However, it is inevitable that we will feel lonely when the union of spirits is broken by illicit sexual relations. Loneliness is the emotion of isolation and seclusion, which includes a feeling of unfulfillment and incompleteness. It is usually manifested by a mood of sadness, though it may quickly regress into a state of fear and insecurity.

A wife had lived apart from her husband for five months due to his ongoing affair. She told me that she was staying involved with as many activities as she could but was having difficulty shaking the tremendous emptiness.

"Les, I love my husband and I want him back. I know God will take care of me as His Word promises, but that truth seems so hard to grasp. Every night I hate going to bed because I feel so completely alone." She worried that she would be unable to fill the hole created by the absence of her husband.

This woman's anguish is a common part of the grief experienced by the injured mate. Like others in similar plights, she likened her lifestyle as "stumbling aimlessly through a fog." What used to have meaning becomes trivial. What once brought happiness is met with disinterest. While the support of friends and family is helpful, it falls short of ultimate relational needs. Future goals seem insignificant as the mind becomes focused on making it through one day.

Loneliness, when experienced in the extreme, leads to one of two unhealthy behavior patterns: excessive isolation or excessive clinging. In isolation, individuals want nothing to do with former relationships. Perhaps feeling very embarrassed or ashamed, they will not allow themselves to be supported. They do not talk about their feelings or needs to anyone. Instead they build a thick wall of protection around themselves, vowing to keep anyone from inflicting further misery.

The other pattern is excessive clinging. The loneliness is so overwhelming that some actively seek people who allow them to cry on their shoulders. They will dominate conversations with obsessive rambling about personal woes. They may feel desperate to find a new partner of the opposite sex who will fill the void created by the departed spouse.

If the injured mates determine not to succumb to total defeat these extremes can be avoided. They will never relish lonely feelings, yet they can determine not to be overwhelmed by them.

Depression

At times anger and loneliness become so prominent that an injured mate sinks into persistent depression. More than deep sadness, depression is an emotion of defeat and hopelessness. It is manifested by an inability to handle normal lifestyle requirements, unexplained crying spells, chronic fatigue, sleep irregularities, poor concentration, and a loss of motivation. Acute anxiety and nervousness often accompany depression. An inclination toward depression is a normal part of grief, but a full pattern of this emotion does not have to occur. When it does, it usually indicates a preexisting propensity toward fragile emotions. The mate's affair is the event that draws the individual over the line.

The most distinguishing factor of depression is unresolved anger. The depressed person has many ideas about how one should have been treated more fairly, but because those ideas are not openly explored they turn into the sour disposition of depression. The thoughts of the individual, which are invariably negative and frustrated must be monitored to identify the link between anger and depression.

Depression is also brought on by struggles with feelings of inferiority. A sense of devaluation is strong. So are the feelings of failure and inadequacy. At times the possibility of returning to a normal life seems so remote that it is easier to collapse in despair. The depressed person will likely use the word *can't* repeatedly. This signals that he or she has given up on the possibility that God can salvage the situation. Depressed persons in this state of mind frustrate family and friends by their stubborn refusal to be helped.

In some cases depression reaches such proportions that it negatively affects the individual's physiological makeup. Gastrointestinal problems may appear, and there may be problems with constipation. Headaches can be frequent. Sleep irregularities can occur. Rapid heartbeat may develop, as can severe anxiety attacks. The body can suffer a depletion of the brain amines norepinephrine or serotonin, creating what might be called a chemical depression, which calls for the use of antidepressant medicines. These symptoms indicate an extreme difficulty in accepting circumstances which causes the emotions to be released somatically.

MANAGING GRIEF SUCCESSFULLY

When a person is forced to contend with the many emotions associated with a mate's affair, the goal is not to eliminate painful feelings. That does not realistically acknowledge one's humanness. The goal is to successfully manage those feelings. In fact, the Lord Himself is not immune to holy grief, as expressed by instructions in Ephesians 4:30 to refrain from grieving the Holy Spirit.

In counseling Ron, we focused on three major problems which hindered his ability to successfully grieve: dependency, control, and abrasiveness.

Dependency

Ron and I discussed how he let Laura dictate his emotions. If she was pleasant, he felt calm. If she sulked, he became angry. If she was cool, he felt insecure.

"Ron, it seems as though you have handed her the controls to your emotions, and depending on which button she pushes, your moods fluctuate."

He chuckled, "Never before would I have described myself as dependent. But you're right. I've let her play god, though she can't possibly be relied upon to be my all in all."

I smiled as we talked. "Don't think of yourself as abnormal. We all have dependencies, even the gruffest macho men. I think everyone would agree that we feel better when we are liked and worse when rejected. The goal is not to get rid of dependencies but to determine how to keep emotions from the extremes when a loved one fails us."

Ron began planning how to maintain composure whether or not Laura was supportive. On evenings when she was irritable he would respond with patience. When she was aloof, he would think of his value before God. If she was uncooperative, he would take on a firm but gentle disposition.

Control

Ron and I examined the issue of control in his response to Laura's affair. We agreed that he was asking for increased heartache if he attempted to force her to act or feel in pre-scribed ways. He acknowledged her God-given free will, although he didn't necessarily like it. He also understood that human nature tends to respond to control with rebellion.

"It is difficult to let her be what she is when I disagree with the way she is handling her life." But Ron understood that God Himself offers free will, so he could not expect to maintain composure by acting counter to God. When Ron let go of the need for control he was not as susceptible to strong anger, and Laura was more willing to loosen up on her tight emotions.

Abrasiveness

Ron was by nature a take-charge person; he wanted to express limits *so* firmly and rigidly that Laura could not mistake his desires. Ron and I determined that the more abrasively he expressed himself, the more he assured a continuation of un-wanted frustration. By lowering his voice he was heard more readily. Such discipline felt awkward, but Ron's goal was not to become an emotional wreck.

Ron and I did not lose sight of reality throughout this healing process. He slipped from his game plan occasionally, but we recognized this as predictable. Ron regretted the strain that developed in his marriage, but he felt grateful that it caused him to learn new ways to handle his emotions.

The following are helpful suggestions for the spouse frustrated by the adultery of the mate.

DON'T BE SURPRISED BY THE WIDE-RANGING EMOTIONS

One morning a woman called me in panic: "It's been two weeks since my husband's affair was discovered, and I keep wondering when my highs and lows will end!"

I asked her to express how she had felt in the last couple of days, and her reply was a common one: "I have times when I handle matters very rationally and am as calm as normal. But sometimes my emotions are sparked by just a look from my husband. I may get an empty aching inside or be tempted to charge toward him in a blind rage. I have no way of knowing which side of my personality will emerge."

We are emotional creatures and emotions can surface so rapidly that they may outpace the mind's ability to make sense of them. This is doubly true when we are under duress. The person who claims exemption from strong negative emotion has not yet been exposed to circumstances which evoke it.

Once an affair is discovered no predictable pattern of emotions can be expected. *The only predictable thing is the emotion's unpredictable nature.* Some people may have a powerful initial struggle with anger followed by an unnatural insecurity. Others may feel such an overwhelming loneliness that they can barely muster the energy to become angry. Still others will experience a chronic bewilderment that leaves them walking in a daze, shaking their heads as they vainly attempt to make sense of all that has happened. Not one of these reactions is more correct than another. It is quite normal to have experiences that seemingly break the mold, since *there is no mold*.

ALLOW HEALTHY EXPRESSIONS OF THESE EMOTIONS

Individuals who handle an affair least effectively are those who attempt to prove that they are immune to emotional frailties. One man's wife abruptly announced that she was having an affair and would be seeking a divorce. This husband showed no feelings of hurt, probably afraid that he might appear weak or needy. When a friend asked how he was handling his adjustments, he shrugged and stated, "These things happen. You just learn to move on." When his adult sons expressed strong sadness over the loss of their mother, he derided them for being too sensitive. About eight months after his wife's announcement, this same man was referred to me by a physician friend. He had developed ulcers, his blood pressure was unstable, and his sleep erratic. I told this man that it was okay to express hurting emotions. The first two or three sessions he maintained his tough veneer, but by our fourth discussion he broke down with deep sobbing as he told me how painful it felt to be rejected by his wife. He could have saved himself much agony and bitterness had he expressed these emotions earlier.

There is no shame in feeling or sharing these emotions with others. Galatians 6:2 encourages Christians to share problems: "Bear one another's burdens, and so fulfill the law of Christ." By expressing emotions we allow ourselves to be ministered to by others, thus increasing a sense of Christian community.

At times people hesitate to share feelings because they do not want to be whiners or blamers. It is good to be wary of the temptation to go overboard; this can be offensive to others as well as increase the tendency to be self-centered. However, a balanced expression of emotions can release building pressure and eliminate the potential for extreme reactions.

Persons finding themselves "blocking" emotions can learn to write out their feelings. Putting thoughts on paper can be invaluable in identifying and clarifying inner conflicts. Then they can be shared with a mature friend, a minister, or Christian counselor.

ULTIMATE EMOTIONAL HEALING IS POSSIBLE, INDEPENDENT OF THE SPOUSE

Innumerable verses in Scripture address lifestyle habits, attitudes, emotional stability, and communication practices. Not one is accompanied by the phrase *if other humans treat us right*. People cannot be relied on to be consistent or steady in times of real strain, therefore God never requires people to look to even closest family members for empowerment. Instead, Jesus said: "Come to Me, all you who labor and are heavy laden, and I will give you rest" (Matt. 11:28). He alone is our sustenance.

Make no mistake, God desires that human relationships be a source of joy and contentment, but the influence of sin is so strong that He has offered Himself as the "safety net" to fall upon. This means that it is necessary to find friendships and support groups to soothe hurting emotions, but the ultimate route toward emotional healing is internal, based on a reliance on God. The apostle Paul underscored this in Philippians 4:11: "I have learned in whatever state I am, to be content."

Many injured spouses get stuck in a groove of unresolved grief by insisting that the mate should hear their feelings then change. There are no guarantees that a new and improved relationship can be established—even after perfectly expressing needs with the mate. Open confrontations could lead to genuine change but may not. Open sharing of concerns should proceed for the sake of personal cleansing with the hope of a better pattern of marital interchange, but with the determination that healing will occur however the mate responds.

Even in the most difficult circumstances an individual has choices. Injured mates cannot choose what the spouse will or will not do, but they can choose their own lifestyle and emotions. Those desiring personal stability will sift through the options, even if the mate chooses a course of instability.

DO WHAT YOU CAN EXTERNALLY TO HELP THE CIRCUMSTANCES

Making personal peace internally and spiritually does not mean abandoning external options. For example, when a mate has an affair, the family lifestyle should be examined for any negative contributions toward tension. If a particular social group has had negative influences, it should be avoided. If alcohol has created too loose a home atmosphere, it can be eliminated. If schedules allow little time for pleasant husband-wife communication, these can be altered. If church participation has been lacking, it can be increased. Many other external adjustments can also be a part of emotional healing.

One woman told me that she could not change what had happened but she considered her husband's adultery to be a signal that something needed to be different in her life. She examined all aspects of her lifestyle—time spent with the children, the social calendar, personal devotion time, family communication patterns, spending habits—and decided that by playing supermom she had avoided some of her marital needs. She whittled down her children's activities so that she had more free time at home each evening. She watched less TV and focused more attention on her husband. She put herself on a budget, knowing that her loose spending habits had annoyed her husband for years. And she vowed to keep telephone conversations brief. Her story follows:

"When the news broke, I was devastated. I felt both angry and confused. I felt like I had no foundation for personal worth. After moping for several weeks, I decided that the best way to respond to our problem was to restructure my way of living so it would be more suitable to clean emotions. In a strange way, the problem became a positive boost that made me examine myself as never before."

Keep in mind that changing external matters is only helpful up to a certain point. Ultimately, inner attitudes and commitments will determine a rewarding life. But adjusting the environment as much as reality will allow makes sense.

STAY IN TOUCH WITH ROUTINE ACTIVITIES

When a person grieves over troubles within the marriage it is tempting to withdraw from normal activities and become self-preoccupied. It is normal to slow the pace of the daily routine during grief, but it is best to keep in touch with many elements of normal life.

One man spoke to me regarding the way he handled his reaction to his wife's leaving him for another man. Naturally he felt hurt and rejected when he uncovered her adulterous relationship, and he initially reacted with explosive anger. When she suggested that they both seek counseling, he cursed and cynically told her to get counseling with her boyfriend. She decided to live apart from him, and his anger turned into bitter depression. He did the bare minimum to keep in touch with his daily routine. He went to work and did what he had to do to get by, although he admits being ineffective. Beyond that, he withdrew from friends, stopped attending church, let the house stay messy, and quit his exercise regimen. For a year or more he merely existed.

He later realized he had lost a large piece of his adult life that could never be retrieved. "I know that I needed time to let my emotions settle, but I went too far. I almost stopped being a normal man."

During grief, emotions may be felt so strongly that it seems as if normalcy cannot be recaptured. But our minds are powerful enough to veto emotional extremes when higher priorities are pursued. This does not mean that feelings have to be repressed. Rather, they can be held in check long enough to maintain daily responsibilities. The transition back into a fuller life will not be as imposing by keeping in touch with normal activities.

The greatest healing occurs when the jilted spouse witnesses a transformation in the unfaithful mate. In some cases this never happens, and divorce may be the result. But in situations where the straying mate is willing, I expend much energy encouraging insight into that person.

At this point in the healing process, I try to get the unfaithful spouse to enter counseling so he or she can understand the dynamics of the affair. If this does not happen, I still encourage the injured spouse to sift through the whys of the affair. This can promote personal growth and tie up the loose ends caused by the confusing turn of events.

Part 2 of this book examines the factors that push an unfaithful spouse into rebellious behavior so that the couple can understand what happened and can deal with these problems, either separately or together.

PART 2
Why Infidelity Occurs

4

Unresolved Anger

Mel was a happy-go-lucky guy who could shoot the breeze with anyone. He was always ready with a joke or funny story and could instantly put people at ease.

Mel came in for counseling at the request of his wife, but did not seem to take counseling very seriously. He wore a big grin that communicated a chronically frivolous approach to life. Flippantly, he said, "Ask me anything you want, Doc. I'm an open book."

When I asked him to describe the activities surrounding his affair he casually explained, "Hey, what can I say? In this day and age these things happen. I can't say that I was really happy at home, but I wasn't looking for an affair either. It just happened."

We discussed his marriage and he admitted that he and his wife of six years had less-than-perfect communication. He was a salesman in a retail store and his wife, Debbie, worked as a bank secretary. She had three teenage children by a previous marriage and seemed preoccupied by them. Aside from work Mel busied himself with an active participation in sports leagues. He had a hard time describing his emotions related to his wife. So I had to identify some of the particulars for him. It was obvious that we would need to examine his anger since he repeatedly referred to frustration in their communications.

No one would identify Mel as a volatile, irritable person. He stated, "I may have my share of problems, but anger isn't one of them." But Mel was an adulterer. He had been divorced and remarried, and in each marriage he had been sexually unfaithful. In both marriages there was a lack of bickering and shouting. Mel would express his displeasures either by leaving the house or by making sarcastic, joking remarks to shut down arguments.

I suggested to Mel that we examine how anger played a part in his adulterous relationships. He seemed genuinely surprised. "Doc, I've already told you that I'm not one to erupt; never have been. I get frustrated every now and then but I don't get angry."

His comments did not dissuade me from my desire to explore his anger. Mel, as many others, had a superficial understanding of this emotion.

People do not need to shout, curse, and slam doors to be angry. Anger includes such behaviors, but it is not that one-dimensional. Just as there are many hues of the color blue, there are many shades of anger. Angry expressions range from loud explosions to minor irritations. Included in anger are criticism, annoyance, frustration, hurt, bitterness, resentment, laziness, impatience, envy, jealousy, pet peeves, and even depression. The mind must be stretched to understand anger and recognize how broad it really is.

I have never seen a case of infidelity without accompanying anger. In some cases the anger is evident. However, in many cases it is very subtle, requiring some astute reading between the lines. The decision to become involved in an affair represents an act of rebellion. The conscience warns, "Don't do this, it will lead to trouble." But the rebellious nature retorts: "I don't care what I've been told, I'm going to do it anyway." Such rebellion won't occur without an emotional push, and the emotion most closely linked to rebellion is anger.

DEFINING ANGER

Anger can be understood as the emotion of self-preservation. It occurs in response to criticism, alienation, misunderstanding, rejection, invalidation, or some other negative communication. When anger is aroused, it prompts the individual to take a stand for personal worth, needs, and convictions. The angry person wishes to communicate, "Hey, treat me with respect." Or "Notice that I have legitimate needs which should be met more appropriately." Or "I have convictions that will not allow me to remain neutral about your actions." In one sense, anger performs the healthy function of righting wrongs. Ephesians 4:26 says, "Be angry, and do not sin." Some incidences should evoke the emotion of self-preservation.

Problems abound, though, because (1) anger can be easily entangled with sinful nature and (2) most people are not skilled in distinguishing legitimate and illegitimate expressions of anger. Unfaithful spouses, in particular, may have had a difficult time expressing anger openly or constructively. As a result, many develop patterns of avoiding it or storing it up.

HOW ANGER RELATES TO ADULTERY

Individuals engaged in infidelity are unlikely to have scowls on their faces. In fact, there may be an abundance of smiles and laughter. Some have stated that during the time spent in the affair they felt more relaxed than they had in years. So it might be easy to dismiss anger as playing a part in the activity. One thing must be understood about humans: We are very skilled at hiding emotions, not only from others but from ourselves as well. This is particularly true during a commitment to a lifestyle of deception.

The anger related to unfaithfulness is unresolved tension within a current or previous relationship. In most cases adulterers, like Mel, express futility regarding their marriage. They cite incompatible personalities or consistently unfruitful communications. They recall feeling hurt or frustrated, followed by failed efforts to resolve the problems. Because this increases tension, the need for self-preservation escalates. Since early efforts to hash out problems were futile, substitute forms of self-preservation are sought.

Mel never learned to constructively express his anger with his wife. He might occasionally lash out at her with harsh threats, but normally he would suppress his anger and leave home to "blow off some steam" with his friends. Not surprisingly, he told me that his father had a similar style of handling frustrations. Consequently, Mel was unable to benefit from parental instruction regarding healthy ways of communicating his needs. As an adult Mel's anger was rarely resolved. This caused him to rationalize why it was necessary to do whatever he wanted for self-gratification.

"Mel, I'm beginning to realize that you've never had anyone to talk with about handling anger. Apparently your mother or father didn't give you any instruction."

"If I got mad, I learned real fast how unproductive it was to let anyone know about it."

"How did you handle your emotions when you felt upset?"

"I became the class clown. I was always the one who could put people at ease. I never let myself get upset."

"In the meantime you stored up one unresolved issue after another."

"I guess I must have done that. Now when someone in my family doesn't pay attention to my needs, I still keep it inside. It gives me an excuse to carouse or play around."

The sin nature (goaded by Satan) encourages the individual to consider preserving self's worth or needs by finding someone to love in the way the spouse is supposed to love. Angry thoughts (perhaps muted, perhaps obvious) persist within the mind: "It bugs me that my mate won't give me what I need. I'll just have to do something to preserve what's rightfully mine. I don't care if it's right or wrong, I'm *not* going to continue living in misery!"

Another scenario involves unresolved tensions from childhood. A common example is the person who feels resentful toward a parent who did not properly extend love or rarely gave messages of complete acceptance. The individual with such a deficiency nurses angry thoughts such as: "I don't know when it will happen, but one day I'm going to have the satisfaction of being with someone who will notice me. I don't care if I have to break a few rules to get it."

One woman told me how she went against her best judgment and married the man her parents wanted for her. Later she had an affair, which prompted her to grudgingly state, "You can give my parents credit for this; they kept me under wraps my entire childhood. I decided that it was about time to prove that I have my personal rights, whether they like it or not."

During extensive counseling she explored her habit of letting repressed anger fester. She eventually realized that unfaithfulness was a major problem, but anger was the deeper one.

The Fallacy of Adultery as Anger Relief

Unfaithful spouses often have understandable reasons for their emotions. Just because the behavior is wrong, it should not be assumed that the frustrations are unwarranted. For example, Mel explained how he had quietly tolerated condescending communication from his parents. He married hoping to find relief, but Debbie turned out to have a similar communication style. She criticized him for his style of dress. She was annoyed by his friends. When he asked Debbie to consider a kinder communication style, she quickly retorted that he had no business talking with her that way. He recalled similar criticisms he had received from his parents.

Mel's unseen rage about the injustice of it all burned inwardly. When a different kind of woman showed interest in him, he succumbed to an affair. His bitterness caused him to excuse the sinfulness.

Mel was not completely wrong in feeling angry, but he erred in his immature style of handling the emotion. There were better options than adultery. He could have sought support from understanding male friends; he could have spent more time in his hobbies; or he could have considered counseling to determine a more internal, spiritual route to personal contentment.

Each person will have moments when anger is a normal reaction; our world is imperfect and often insensitive. Mel's situation is a prime example of partially justifiable anger. Yet committing adultery, no matter how frustrated a person may be, is never a good release for anger.

Adultery is sin

The adulterous person, like Mel, is attempting to relieve frustration via a self-centered act. The desire for relief is fine. But healthy anger should be aimed at arousing a response in others that leads to spiritual growth within the relationship. It is impossible to produce growth and repentance through sinful initiatives. This would be analogous to watering flowers with poison.

Whenever anger is released through an act of sin, negative emotions are compounded—every act of sin has a consequence. By God's design, the consequences of sin generate *more* frustration. His hope is that individuals acknowledge the senseless nature of sin and return to righteous ways. A person like Mel who seeks to relieve anger or any other emotion with an act of sin only asks for more problems.

The person expressing anger with sin is becoming more vulnerable to Satan's influence. After the apostle Paul warned the Ephesians, "Be angry, and do not sin," he goes on to say, "Do not let the sun go down on your wrath, *nor give place to the devil*" (Eph. 4:26-27, *italics added*).

Adultery leads to escalating anger

Consider how touchy an individual feels when protecting a very sensitive subject. For example, I know a man who failed the second grade, but he still winces whenever he is reminded of it. To him it has never been a laughing matter, and it never will be. Most of us do not like our weaknesses.

This touchy feeling is extremely common in people like Mel. They know how volatile the atmosphere would be if their conduct became known, so they are very edgy if another person discovers the truth. Individuals who believe that adultery is a good release for long-standing frustrations should think again. Promiscuous conduct gives someone like Mel one more major reason to feel tense, leading to a greater tendency toward passive, sneaky anger or open, verbal hostility.

Adultery hurts others

Mel was not consciously thinking: "I hope this will destroy my wife because I want to make her suffer." True, adultery is often done in spite or vengeance, but the use of deception indicates that harm to the mate is usually secondary to self-pleasure. In fact, people like Mel live with the philosophy that "What others don't know won't hurt them." Nonetheless, harm is being done to the spouse since any diversion from marital growth is a detriment. The spouse may feel the pain of isolation even before an affair is discovered.

To harm someone else in the process of satisfying personal needs is disruptive. When the mate is hurt, the promiscuous spouse loses. This would be akin to the doubles tennis player who wants to avenge the fact that the partner is not playing the preferred style. Rather than discussing how to successfully blend their strategies, the frustrated partner repeatedly trips the other. Perhaps dominance or punishment is conveyed, but the team loses.

One woman said that she specifically sought an affair because her husband was so preoccupied with his work and unattentive to her needs that she developed an "I'll show you" attitude. When her infidelity was uncovered she was surprised at the hurt expressed by her husband.

"I still maintain that I had a legitimate gripe. But in retrospect I see that I could have shared my anger more constructively," this woman admitted. "By striking out in an affair I proved my point, but it created more pain in him than I thought it would. Now I have a new problem [his hurt] that I had never really intended."

Adultery is an external solution for an internal problem

The roots that feed adultery are very deep and multifaceted. If anger is to be understood as the preservation of self-worth, needs, and convictions, the resolution of anger involves much soul-searching about *internal* issues related to personal goals and thought processes. In Mel's case, it meant that he had to be more honest with himself about the insecurities that underlaid his anger. He had developed such a strong need for self-preservation that his insecurities directed his behaviors.

When a person chooses to relieve anger by committing adultery, the anger is not likely to abate since this is a superficial method of problem solving. A change of scenery can be helpful in some situations, but ultimately troublesome emotions can only be resolved via restructured mental processes. Romans 12:2 teaches that transformation arises from the renewing of the mind. I used this process in counseling persons like Mel.

WAYS WE SHOW ANGER

Many of us are not consciously aware of the choices we make; however, we cannot assume that anger is merely a reflex reaction with no preceding thought. (For example, the person who screams obscenities may not consciously think, "Well, let's try obnoxious shouting as a means of venting my anger." Yet close scrutiny of the mind indicates that a split-second, subconscious decision was made to let the anger fly.) In order to thoroughly comprehend anger, it is helpful to examine the choices we make in handling anger.

Repression

When a negative incident occurs, prompting the desire to take a stand of self-preservation, it is possible to squelch the emotion to the extent that it *appears* that there is no feeling of anger. The repression of anger is evidenced when people pretend that all is well when in fact it is not. Examples of this include:

- From previous experiences a wife feels that it is futile to tell her husband her needs; therefore, when his behavior is distasteful, she goes about her normal routine, pretending that she can handle her hurt with no problems at all.
- A wife is dissatisfied with the social plans her husband has made, but when he asks her to finalize the arrangements, she smiles and says, "Sure, no problem."
- A husband doesn't like his wife's manner of managing money. He says something to her once or twice. When that proves fruitless he shrugs but continues to brood about it.
- The communication in a marriage is poor, but instead of discussing ways to improve, the spouses silently suffer as a "gruesome twosome."

These examples illustrate that the repression of anger is never constructive. Repression may temporarily avert an unpleasant interchange, but it also causes an emotional logjam. In many cases the need to stand for personal worth, needs, or convictions is appropriate, yet the anger remains hidden.

Aggressive Anger

The repression of anger eventually causes the acts of self-preservation to be handled in an aggressive manner. Aggressive anger is defined as taking a stand for personal worth, needs, and convictions at someone else's expense. This form of anger is most common in distressed relationships. It is accompanied by inconsideration and rarely leads to successful conflict resolution. Instead it keeps repeating itself in a nonending cycle.

The most obvious manifestation of this type of anger is open aggression. Typical expressions include shouting, criticism, bickering, intimidating, griping, complaining, sarcasm, and condescension. In each instance the individual attempts to take a stand for self-preservation (sometimes legitimate, sometimes not), but it is destructive rather than constructive.

A more subtle form of aggressive anger is passive-aggressive communication. Keep in mind that destructive anger does not have to be expressed in loud or obvious ways. The need for self-preservation coupled with a quietly inappropriate manner of communication may lead to a "behind the scenes" style of anger. Examples of this include the silent treatment, hidden activities, failure to deliver a promised task, and evasiveness. The ultimate goal of each of these is preserving the person's own worth, needs, or convictions with the least amount of vulnerability.

Mel's unfaithfulness was an expression of passive-aggressive anger. He and Debbie had not successfully shared their needs with each other in ways that led to constructive agreements, so he developed a pattern of pouting and withdrawal. Then he talked to himself about how he deserved better treatment. He fantasized about happier circumstances until he was convinced that he was justified in seeing another woman. By the time he started seeing his new girlfriend his anger had a different appearance than it did in his pouting moments. But it was this unresolved emotion that prompted his behind-the-scenes escapades.

Assertive Anger

One of the healthiest means of handling anger is assertiveness. (This assumes that the issue which prompts self-preserving behavior is legitimate.) Assertive anger is defined as taking a stand for personal worth, needs, and convictions while also being constructive and considerate of other people's needs. This form of anger should be used judiciously. James 1:19 cautions us to be "slow to wrath." Assertiveness is not the same as pushiness as some have thought.

There are flaws in every relationship that prompt moments of anger. Healthy persons do not relish the idea of expressing assertive anger, but view it as an act of responsibility. Forms of assertiveness include:

- Setting time limits on events that are not mutually enjoyed.
- Saying no when necessary.
- Requesting legitimate favors.
- Stating opinions firmly, particularly when not previously heard.
- Addressing problems in the open.
- Asking questions when confused.

I first helped Mel identify his moments of anger.

"Mel, I know that you think of anger as being accompanied by shouting or rage. Since you tend not to communicate in that way, it is easy to avoid identifying your anger. Let's first focus on feelings of frustration or annoyance since these are a part of your anger system. When do you notice these types of emotional reactions?"

"Lots of times. Debbie seems content to work all day and then talk on the phone all evening with her friends. That really bugs me. Or one of the kids gets into my workshop in the garage and I can't find my tools. Little irritations like that happen all the time."

"What do you usually do in those moments?"

"Usually nothing. I've learned that it doesn't do much good to state my opinions, so I generally don't make a fuss."

"Then afterward you are stewing inwardly."

"You got it. I don't know what to do about it, though. Screaming at my family or throwing a fit won't do any good. That's why I do nothing."

The next step in teaching Mel to deal with anger was to help him express his anger appropriately so it would not go underground.

"Wait a minute. You always have choices, no matter how difficult your situation may seem. Let's take a look at an example. How would your wife respond if you asked her to set aside some time away from the phone each evening in order to spend time with you? Would she do it?"

"Who knows?"

"Have you tried?"

"Maybe. But probably not like I should."

Mel and I went on to discuss how to explain to his wife that he would like her to address his needs. He first had to admit that his annoyances would turn into a greater type of anger if left unchecked. And he knew that he would have to work at maintaining a gentleness in his voice. Also, he should state his preference succinctly, to avoid confusing Debbie with unnecessary rambling. In time, as he refused to allow the anger to be suppressed unnaturally, he experienced a tremendous release of pressure. By communicating anger assertively, Mel did not have to shout or speak rudely to make his point. Yet close examination indicated that self-preserving measures were being enacted, thus qualifying them as forms of anger.

A major difference between assertive and aggressive anger is that assertiveness typically leads to more immediate conflict resolution. An analogy can be made to pulling up weeds while they are very small, having shallow roots. Expressing dissatisfaction in its early stages is much easier than trying to rid yourself of anger that has had time to grow and tangle itself around all your thoughts.

Releasing Anger

There are times when individuals feel legitimate needs of self-preservation, but the circumstances prohibit a successful exchange of assertiveness. This may be caused by a relationship that is unequal in its level of psychological or spiritual maturity, or by the inability to talk with the person involved in the anger (toward a deceased person for instance). In such a scenario it is unnecessary to repress the anger which only feeds bitterness or depression.

In a later session, Mel shared that recently he had been perfect in expressing assertiveness with Debbie, but on this particular day she didn't respond well. "You would have been proud of me, Doc," he reported. "I was bugged because she came home griping for no reason, so I calmly asked her to relax and ease up on her complaints. I even fixed supper to pacify her. But she was determined to have her mood."

We were able to chuckle with each other because he was describing one of those scenes that every married person can appreciate. "Mel, do you suppose that at those times you can decide to let go of your frustrations and accept her bad mood?"

"A year ago I would have said, 'No way!' But I see your point. I do a lot less fretting than I did then. There's no use in worrying about something that's just going to happen!"

A choice can be made to let the anger go so that its conclusion is fully given to God. This would be consistent with the message of Ephesians 4:31 which instructs us to "put away" problems related to distasteful anger. Contrary to repressed anger, released anger leaves the individual feeling inwardly clean, making kindness and forgiveness possible.

Examples of this include:

- A wife realizes that her husband will never get along well with her family. In spite of many efforts to talk with him about this attitude, he does not change. So rather than bearing a grudge she accepts him as he is.
- A wife is reminded of a husband's mistake from several

years past. They have discussed the problem thoroughly, yet her memories still bring occasional disillusionment. But rather than getting caught in an anger trap she decides to let go of her need for perfect closure and continues to relate normally to him.

- A husband is wise enough to know that everyone has some annoying habits. So rather than hounding his wife about hers, he accepts her as she is.
- A major argument goes unresolved, but the spouses conclude that in lieu of letting resentments fester, they will forgive each other and focus on the matters that *can* be agreed upon.

The release of anger can only be accomplished by persons with inner security. These people recognize that while it is always preferable to have a pleasant environment, emotional composure can exist even when it is unpleasant. No person must be a prisoner to anger when a spouse is less than compatible.

My greatest breakthroughs with Mel came when he first realized that he had a problem with anger and then when he accepted responsibility for it. Rather than looking for his wife or for a girlfriend to relieve him of his frustrations, he began making choices about ways to respond to annoyances without disrupting his moral commitments.

STRATEGIES FOR SUCCESSFUL ANGER RESOLUTION

The best way to control anger is to devise a system of communication that the entire family can share. However, there is still hope if family members are committed to inappropriate or closed communication. Anger resolution may not be as easy, but with proper mental focus and with God's guidance, the anger can become balanced.

Distinguish Essential from Nonessential Issues

For years I have heard people laughingly debate whether rolls of toilet tissue should roll from the top or the bottom—although I had never met a couple who was really serious about it. However, a couple recently came seeking counseling about the husband's unfaithfulness, and within minutes they were blasting away about the other's stubbornness regarding toilet tissue! Accusations of insensitivity were thrown at each other as each ripped brutally into the other's character flaws:

"Don't you even know how to properly install toilet tissue? You should put it so that it unfolds from the top. It's easier to reach that way!" the husband said.

"That shows how much you know. When you fix it to unfold from the bottom, it's easier to tear. But I can't expect you to use such simple logic."

"Yeah, well you're a fine one to talk about logic. What's logical about not replacing an empty roll of toilet tissue like you should have done last week? You're so irresponsible!"

"You don't know what you're talking about. Besides, if I did replace it you'd criticize me for doing it the wrong way!"

Many people get mad about items that fall into the "who cares?" category. Their need for self-preservation is so keen that even the smallest disputes elicit an emotional response. One man, reflecting on the days prior to an extended affair, admitted that he felt justified in his sexual sin because of his anger, yet he could hardly remember anything truly significant that deserved the emotion that dominated him. His anger would be provoked by simple things: his wife wore the "wrong" dress, she was four minutes late for an event, an employee made an error filling out an invoice, his son's ball game interrupted a TV show. Many picky incidences created frustration; he was a time bomb waiting to explode. So he developed an "I've got to get even" attitude and began pleasing personal desires in whatever fashion suited him.

Ephesians 4:26 gives a go-ahead in the expression of anger, but should be understood in conjunction with James 1:19: "Let every man be swift to hear, slow to speak, slow to wrath." Standing up for personal needs is only good when circumstances truly warrant it. I suggested that the couple arguing about toilet tissue simply accept minor irritants as a natural part of cohabitation. This meant that they would set aside pet peeves so the marriage would not choke on tiny problems. At first they reluctantly agreed. In time they learned that it really didn't matter if each small disagreement was left at loose ends.

Anger should be reserved for convictions regarding morality or righteousness, problems involving personal abuse, matters of extreme insensitivity, and gross neglect of legitimate needs. Like the boy who cried wolf, the person who overuses anger will not be taken seriously and will be left holding much emotional garbage.

Discuss Your Needs Openly

In most marriages touched by adultery, personal needs are not well addressed—they go unexpressed or are expressed so offensively that they may as well have been left unsaid. For example, Mel and his wife determined to keep each other informed of legitimate needs and desires. Mel, in particular, had never felt comfortable in exposing himself this way, yet he wanted to remedy previous flaws.

As they explained the positive effects of this new habit, the two spoke as if they had made the discovery of the century: "In the past we either walled each other out or bantered in accusing tones. Now that we have committed to sharing our feelings constructively we can laugh at the foolishness of our old ways.

"We have virtually no stored-up anger because we keep a clean slate. The reward is a higher level of trust than we have ever known."

Mel and his wife gave several examples of constructively discussing their needs:

- Instead of pushing her point of view with the expectation of an immediate reaction, Debbie learned to state her needs and let her husband have some time to mull over his response before resolutions were discussed.
- Realizing his wife's desire for a reaction when she expressed a need, Mel committed to be more frank in telling her how he felt.
- Instead of accusing each other with sentences beginning "You should . . . ," they decided to speak more personally by stating "I am feeling . . ."
- Mel and Debbie realized that there was more than one answer to each problem, so they committed to being open-minded when seeking conflict resolution.

Discussing personal needs may not produce immediate feelings of ease. It forces individuals out of their comfort zones to examine issues that may not be pleasant or flattering. Yet, in the end each spouse feels known and the mystery is removed from the relationship. Trust is enhanced and the need to seek a third party to satisfy frustrations diminishes.

Refrain from Condescension

Remember that the goal of successful anger is self-preservation and a restored relationship. Feelings of both the sender and the receiver need consideration. Therefore a mindset of coequality is best. Any attempt at one-upmanship will be avoided.

Sharing anger in a coequal fashion requires self-restraint. When anger is felt it is usually in response to a less-than-flattering experience such as being ignored or invalidated. And anger often leads to attempts of domination or control because each human tends to compensate for feelings of inadequacy by attempting to make others look inadequate. Power plays are common because an adversarial feeling exists. Consequently, angry exchanges often have a "seesaw" effect—one person speaks down to the other which prompts an attempt to speak condescendingly in reverse.

Mel admitted using derogatory terms when expressing frustrations to his wife. He told me how he once asked his wife, "How can you let the children convince you to spend so much money in buying designer clothes? Don't you have a brain?"

"How did she react?" I asked.

"She told me that if I wanted to look at an idiot I should go stand in front of a mirror."

"Mel, you have legitimate things to say, but you can say them in such condescending ways that your wife misses the point altogether. Try saying something like: 'I'd like to keep the spending down when we buy our children's clothes.'"

Mel knew this was a better approach. He realized that the seesaw style of communication made him want to run. He committed himself to being more reasonable when expressing needs with his wife.

The apostle Paul advises in Ephesians 4:15 to speak the truth in love. This means that personal needs and convictions should be spoken without gaining an upper hand. Firmness can be accompanied by compassion; it can coexist with an attitude of fairness.

Attend to the Spouse's Anger

Fairness dictates that if one partner has the chance to express anger, so should the other. Time can be taken for all sides of an issue to be explored. Contrasting perspectives can be considered. Each couple has different personality qualities; allowances can be made for uniqueness.

Mel and Debbie sat in my office discussing a conversation from the night before. As Mel expressed his perspective on the subject, Debbie would break in with objections. Then it would be his turn to explain why her objections were off base. She would counter with an even more overwhelming comeback.

I let this continue about five minutes, then asked, "Do you suppose this style of expressing anger has anything to do with Mel's decision to look outside the marriage to find someone who would understand?" The answer was obvious.

It may be difficult, but with determination, spouses can give credibility to each other's feelings and perceptions, no matter how far off. For example, Debbie agreed that when Mel had something to say, even if she did not like it or agree with it, she would receive it without rebuttal. "I've never thought of it that way before," she might reply. Likewise, Mel would allow Debbie to express her annoyances with him, and even in instances when he felt she was wildly off track, he would fully acknowledge her perceptions. "Let me take some time to think about what you just said."

When spouses give credibility to each other's feelings they each feel valued and emotions refrain from growing to the point of rage. Objectivity replaces sheer subjectivity, and problems appear manageable.

Know When to Forgive

I have yet to meet a person having an affair who was not holding a grudge. Usually this grudge is against the spouse, though at times it may also be held toward a parent or a past close acquaintance. The affair is a type of reward for the misery the person has endured at the hand of someone else.

The adulterer needs to consider the option of forgiveness to overcome the anger which accompanies a grudge. This forgiveness is not to be construed as something that *must* be done, because if "have to" is the only motivation to forgive, it will probably be phony. Rather, forgiveness is to be understood as a choice. Ephesians 4:31-32 concludes that it is the only good choice if anger is to be set aside in favor of composure: "Let all bitterness, wrath, anger, clamor, and evil speaking be put away from you, with all malice. And be kind to one another, tender-hearted, forgiving one another."

Mel learned to think to himself, "If I really want to, I can hold resentments for years. If I forgive it will be because it is my desire." The New Testament Christian is not legalistically bound to do as Scripture teaches. Consequences are still experienced, but a choice is nonetheless present. If forgiveness occurs, it will be because the individual chooses to yield his or her will to God's ways. In doing so, lingering anger can be laid to rest. (Forgiveness is discussed further in Chapter 12.)

One major cause of infidelity can be set aside by understanding the dynamics of anger and learning to handle it successfully. In the next chapter excessive neediness, another factor in infidelity, will be discussed. It can be resolved similarly to help diminish the potential for unfaithful behavior.

5

Excessive Neediness

As a college student I managed to survive on dorm food, but I never really liked it. Powdered mashed potatoes and canned corn are not an appetizing entree. When I visited my folks' house I ate like a glutton. Nothing compared to Mom's pot roast and vegetable casseroles! Because I lacked meals that satisfied, my craving for her food was enormous.

Promiscuous people may relate to this analogy. In most cases they feel deficient in affection. Because their supply of affection is lacking, they are hungry for anything that might resemble the real thing. Many times their feelings of neediness are real. Sometimes they are imagined or greatly exaggerated. A main feature of their behavior is a craving to be loved or to feel close to a warm body.

One woman, Sandra, explained, "I was tired of going to bed every night feeling desperately lonely. My husband always told me that he was satisfied with our relationship. He never seemed to understand why I wanted more sharing from him."

Sandra's husband was a highly successful businessman who admittedly expended more energy on work than on his family. Each month he spent several nights out of town, and when in town he would leave the house early and come home late, often after the children had gone to bed. Sandra had given up on talking with him about private matters. It had become abundantly clear that he had little interest in personal perspectives or emotions.

"Legally we were married, but we had little sense of union. I was glad to see him leave the house because then I wouldn't be reminded of any pain.

"I'll admit that I would often fantasize about a more caring, romantic relationship. There were times when I would feel the ultimate in frustration because I was capable of dreaming about Mr. Right, but I couldn't really make it happen."

"So when your new man friend came along, you were easily swept off your feet."

"Well, I never let on to anyone that I was enamored with the other man. In fact, we knew each other for over a year before any sparks flew. But once the affair began I felt like a schoolgirl with a gigantic crush."

Love is first among each person's God-given needs. Developmental psychologists have determined that infants who are deprived of normal loving interactions with parents become listless, demotivated, intellectually stunted, and socially dysfunctional. Similarly, adults who do not feel sufficiently loved become depressed or withdrawn. They often take greater risks with morality, their spiritual capacities are depleted, and their inferiority feelings mount.

The Bible has numerous references explaining the need for love. Genesis 2:24 indicates that a man is to cleave to his wife, becoming one flesh. This is often read at wedding ceremonies to emphasize the intense bonding of the marital union. In Matthew 22:37-39 Jesus told us that love for God and love for one's neighbor are the supreme commandments in life. It is no accident that God gives each human a craving for this emotion.

NEEDINESS UNDERLIES ADULTERY

Unfortunately, few people fully comprehend God's commandment to love, and even fewer are skilled in giving love away so that it produces lasting contentment in one's spouse, children, or friends. The inability of others to satisfy legitimate love needs is never an excuse for infidelity, but it does shed light on the reasons for sexual improprieties. I have heard statements like these many times:

- "I felt so tired of being criticized that I had to find relief."
- "My spouse was so busy with other things that it made me feel unimportant."
- "My spouse sure didn't care about *me,* so I didn't care either."
- "Nothing I said was taken seriously."
- "All I wanted was someone who would be kind and who would touch me."
- "My spouse is too easily irritated and I rarely feel like I can do enough to be accepted."

A person wandering through the desert without water or nourishment loses his senses and behaves abnormally. The same is true for the person who wanders through a marriage without perceiving the love necessary for lasting contentment. A person often begins marriage with this feeling of neediness without realizing it.

CHILDHOOD FACTORS RELATED TO NEEDINESS

Often one spouse is predisposed to sexual acting out because of emotional neediness in that person's childhood.

Unloving Family History

In the parent-child family system, God designed the father and mother to love the children in such a way that the children would feel totally accepted and clearly comprehend God the Father's secure love. The fall into sin stained that plan. Many mothers and fathers, aware of their need to set aside sinfulness in favor of God's guidance, make a very good effort to minimize sin's hold on their lives. Their children usually grow up well adjusted. But many parents do not reconcile their ways to the Lord, or if they do, they are inconsistent in letting Him guide each day. Their offspring often develop an aching to be loved, which lingers into the adult years.

Sandra had many positive memories of childhood. She was popular in school, dated as much as she wanted, and was involved in Christian youth groups. Her parents were basically supportive of her outside activities. Yet, one factor stands out in the memory of her early home. She could seldom get her dad to talk with her about anything personal. He was a good provider and spent most evenings at home. But in many respects he was a nonentity to her. That is, he stayed out of the way as Sandra and her sisters engaged in their many activities. He rarely displayed anger or scorn, but he did not display affection either. Sandra recalls many conversations with her sisters as they would complain about dad's noninvolvement and the impossibility of getting him to respond. Their mother, aware of their feelings, could only console them by saying, "I know what you are talking about."

I spoke with Sandra about this. "I have a suspicion that this lack of fatherly love created a hunger in you for male affection."

"I was boy crazy, all right. I never admitted that it was related to Dad's lack of attention, but I would smother any male who showed me gentleness."

"Maybe you weren't consciously attempting to compensate for the lack of paternal love, but your behavior indicates there was an emotional hole you wanted to fill."

"You're right. I remember wishing that I could find someone who would talk with me intimately and give me insight into his feelings . . . just like Dad *didn't* do."

Many times I find that adulterers had a hunger for love dating back to childhood. Perhaps they remember how acceptance was tied to performance. Or they felt that their unique perceptions and feelings were never heard. Maybe they recall that while love was present it was not shared very often. Many remember experiences related to neglect, sexual abuse, harsh punishment, or extreme strictness. Throughout the developmental years a yearning to feel significant grew inwardly. Feeling frustrated in the hope of finding it at home, these people developed a habit of looking elsewhere.

When people grow up in such environments, one of two problems may carry over into marriage: (1) They may marry someone with a similar inability to love fully, which can double the feeling of hopelessness; or (2) They can be so unaccustomed to handling healthy love that no relationship will be good enough.

When these persons choose to become sexually involved outside marriage, they are not necessarily thinking about the need to recapture that childhood love. They are only mindful of the desire to feel satisfied for the moment. Yet close analysis exposes the fact that a feeling of psychological neediness has existed for years. Perhaps it had previously been satisfied through other means, such as achievement or public approval, but finally it became so strong that it had to be satisfied through sexual interplay.

Poor Identity Development

It is common to hear promiscuous adults state, "I just don't know who I am anymore." Perhaps in the past they expended enormous energies satisfying social requirements to be acceptable, but in retrospect it all seemed like a mindless game. Then at the onset of an affair they encounter the dark side of their own personalities. They see in themselves an insecurity or a confusion they had not previously encountered. Such behavior invalidates all their previous beliefs.

This identity confusion can usually be traced to a childhood that did not encourage the individual to seriously struggle with personal beliefs. Beliefs or rules may have been frequently *told to* the developing child, but telling a child what to believe is very different from stimulating a child to grapple with the concepts.

I spoke with Kent, a former pastor in his late thirties, who always seemed to be a bastion of stability. He made very good grades in school. His friends' parents pinpointed him as the role model to emulate. He married his high school sweetheart during college and was told that they looked like the perfect couple. He had many preaching opportunities during his college days which gave him invaluable experience very early, and he had held three very successful pastorates, each typified by numerical growth and broad popularity. But he was derailed because of a sexual relationship he had with a woman in his congregation.

When I asked about his early relationship with his parents he told me, "There was never any question about right and wrong in my family. My parents were kind, godly people, but I knew I couldn't stray from the rules."

"How often did the family gather together for the purpose of sharing unique feelings or ideas or perceptions?" I asked.

"Well, we never shared in the sense you are suggesting. The atmosphere was pretty cut and dried. The kids were told what to do and we knew better than to disagree."

As Kent talked about his affair he sighed deeply and said, "I know what the Bible says, and I honestly believe the Christian way is right. But something caused me to be drawn to this other way of life. I'm not sure what it was."

I attempted to help Kent understand this attraction by explaining that his sense of morality had been told to him rather than drawn from within. For example, he had been bluntly ordered, "I'd better not hear of you getting too flirtatious with a girl," rather than "Let's sit down and discuss your ideas about dating and attractions to girls."

Or he would hear, "If you think you're going to make it in the ministry, you've got to prove that you are willing to witness and take a firm stand for your faith." He told me he would have preferred: "Being in the ministry is a major decision, and I'm interested in hearing your feelings about God's hand on your life." Kent discovered that he had been living correctly for years, but his motivation to do so was external rather than internal.

Living without a well-developed sense of internal controls leaves individuals vulnerable to whims of the moment, particularly those of a sexual nature. They hunger for less conditional relationships. These people lack sufficient reasoning depth to overcome powerful temptations, so they may be drawn into a relationship that promises to be easygoing and fun. Because of

91

the rebellion associated with infidelity, such persons often fail to "find" themselves—the behavior creates more problems than it solves.

Unrealistic Expectations

Becky baffled her family and friends because the attachment to her extramarital sexual partner seemed as strong as an addiction. No amount of reasoning caused her to let go of him. As Becky talked about her background, she described her childhood as "perfect." Her mother was always available, entertaining Becky and her two brothers with stories and fun activities, consistently helping them complete their homework. Her father, although a busy man, was also described as an approachable, understanding man who would do anything for his family.

When Becky married, her husband was good to her but did not give her the same special attention she had come to expect from a family. He might forget to run errands or was snappish when the children disobeyed. Over the years Becky subconsciously nursed the thought that if her husband continued to be imperfect, she deserved to find someone who would better satisfy her needs.

When individuals develop unrealistic expectations, which cause them to be easily dissatisfied with a marital relationship, it can usually be traced to one of two extremes in the developmental years: (1) *The atmosphere was so idealistic that the negative side of life was not sufficiently addressed.* The individual learned that life can be virtually problem free. Others can be leaned upon for personal contentment. They will be more than happy to be totally accommodating; or (2) *The atmosphere at home was in a regular uproar.* Emotional peaks and valleys were so common that a deep weariness grew internally. Fantasies abounded as images of the perfect family soothed painful emotions: "I know there *must* be someone who can give me a better life than this, I just *know* it!" These people have such high hopes for the marriage relationship that anything short of perpetual bliss is considered a bust. An affair is pursued with the hope that it will produce the "ideal" feelings.

When unrealistic expectations are held, personal needs are almost impossible to satisfy. Simple family problems are over-interpreted which magnifies the person's sense of despair and further feeds idealistic dreams.

MINIMIZING EXCESSIVE NEEDINESS

The goal in identifying how adulterers may be acting upon long-standing excessive neediness is not to rid an individual of all neediness but to establish balance. God uses needs as motivators to search for His will in our lives.

As unfaithful spouses learn more about the whys of their behaviors, I hope they will pursue healthier, spiritual alternatives. God is gracious and wants each error to be used as a means to turn to Him. He is ready to provide solutions for all problems. There are several steps required to bring balance to excessive neediness.

STEP #1: Consider Worth to Be a Spiritual Matter.

As my sessions with Sandra (the woman with the inattentive husband) continued, it became clear that she had learned to value herself only if her husband valued her. Since her husband was often emotionally unavailable she felt inadequate much of the time. Add to this her gnawing questions related to her father's love and her vulnerability to infidelity is understandable. She had two options to relieve her emptiness: (1) She could make her husband and father responsible for her feelings of worth, which would force her to either make them fit her mold or find another man who would, or (2) She could learn to make her feelings of worth an internal, spiritual matter anchored in her knowledge and experience of God's love.

Many adults who recall relationships that inadequately addressed love needs frequently use those experiences to excuse sexual misbehaviors: "If others had met my needs more sufficiently, I wouldn't be in the mess I'm in now." But Scripture does not endorse such a mind-set. A person needs to know when to let go of the past and grow in God's strength. The apostle Paul reflected, "When I was a child, I spoke as a child, I understood as a child, I thought as a child; but when I became a man, I put away childish things" (1 Cor. 13:11). Paul acknowledged that the adult mind, guided by God, could become fixed on far greater truths, thus putting to rest the weaknesses developed during childhood years.

To set aside neediness developed in childhood, adults must acknowledge that God gifted each of us with a mind capable of reason and deliberations. Unhealthy habits, subconsciously carried into adulthood, can be relearned to conform to God's desires. For example, Sandra learned to change her mental focus in specific ways:

- When recalling incidences of her father's distancing, she reminded herself that he was an imperfect mortal whose messages did not carry the power of God.
- She chose to show her belief in God's love for her by speaking with confidence to her husband, realizing she did not have to apologize for legitimate needs.
- When her husband was inattentive, she reminded herself that she was looking for a false, external feel-good experience by dreaming about another man's love. No human could be so complete that she would entrust him with her self-worth.

Ultimately, each adult is accountable to choose between the patterns of thought offered by historical experiences versus those offered in scriptural teachings. Many people feel incapable of shedding problems deeply ingrained in the personality. They forget that a function of the Holy Spirit is to strengthen where strength is not humanly found. A commitment can be made to look to God for personal value. Recognition can be given to the historical truth of Jesus' life, death, and resurrection. God's Word can be studied and trusted. By doing so, the decision is made to let emotional neediness be satisfied first and foremost by a relationship with God through Jesus Christ.

STEP #2: Develop a Contemplative Mind.

Once a decision is made to develop spiritual strength to fill the voids of emotional neediness, it is necessary to let the mind become filled with God's wisdom. This requires regular time for study and meditation. Philosophical issues are explored in the attempt to build a sound base of reasoning, which acts as a stabilizer in instances of tension.

My breakthrough with Kent, the former minister, came when he admitted that his Christian values had been told to him with such a strong expectation that he *must* make them his own. He had been living according to his parents' agenda. He hated admitting this because he had been considered a brilliant student with a tremendously creative mind. He had a broad capacity for philosophical thought. Yet he had not gone through the necessary soul-searching and struggle that cause beliefs to become deeply personal. He had learned his way of life by rote memory and imitation.

To solidify his moral beliefs, Kent decided to go back to scratch and make initial evaluations of his guiding principles. He grappled with questions such as:

- Why should I bother to maintain sexual purity? Does it make *that* much difference?
- What does it really mean to be Spirit-guided?
- How sinful is sin? What does it mean to the holy God?
- What does it mean to have self-control? What is its source?
- Do I truly endorse humility?

As he pondered such issues week after week, a feeling of cleanness came over him. "I'm genuinely feeling whole because I know who I am, and my behaviors are far less phony."

I have particular concern for a trend that I call "passive Christianity." We tend to nurse a lazy mind-set regarding spiritual and psychological matters because our secular lives are propped up by the god of convenience. For example, rather than meditating on Scripture in a serious fashion, most Christians go to church each week hoping that the pastor had time to prepare a good sermon. Spiritual growth is a passive exercise contingent upon someone else's effort. It is no wonder that many Christians draw little strength from spiritual precepts when "crunch time" appears. They have let someone else do the digging for them for so long that when it is time to use the shovel, they do not know how to use it.

Excessive neediness is neutralized by a strong sense of self-identity. To accomplish this, personal beliefs of the hand-me-down variety are set aside in favor of those derived from real soul-searching. Others' support and encouragement are still welcome, yet there is a strong anchor of well-conceived ideology to buffer feelings of neediness if that encouragement does not come.

STEP #3: Have Realistic Expectations.

It's fun to fantasize about the perfect life. Yet those who allow fantasies to distract them from the realities of normal marital struggles eventually contend with feelings of disillusionment and emptiness. Strong fantasies lead to unrealistic expectations which in turn inhibit healthy internal stability.

The Bible gives many instructions regarding interpersonal interactions: commands to love, to encourage, to bear another's burdens, to be kind, to confess, and to forgive. The Bible is also clear in explaining the flaws each person is capable of having. It indicates that people can be prone to strife, bitterness, anger, envy, lust, and disputes. Christians are capable of abandoning the negative traits, but no one is completely perfect.

Therefore, expectations of relationships are realistic when balanced by an understanding of the dual nature of mankind. Humans are capable of wonderful fellowship, but they can also be instigators of major frustration. This is heightened in close relationships; these tend to reveal both the best and the worst in us. Realistic persons have normal desires for positive exchanges, but will not be devastated when negatives occur.

I discussed with Sandra that it would be preferable if her husband fit the mold of a perfectly balanced Christian husband. Yet simple fact indicated that he would not.

"You know Sandra, I can't blame you one bit for wanting a husband who will be loving and attentive. In fact, it would be abnormal if you said you *didn't* want him to be sensitive."

"It's good to know that I'm not completely off base in my feelings. But I guess I'll have to get used to the idea of containing my cravings so they won't lead me astray."

"That will be no easy task. But I think you can do it if you restructure your beliefs about your competence to handle adversity."

We then discussed that Sandra's neediness had been heightened by an early lack of training to resolve external problems with a sense of internal confidence. For example, during her teen years when her dad proved to be an inadequate listener, her mother told her, "When you get married, you should be able to talk about your needs much more openly with your husband." So she dreamed endlessly of her shining knight.

Sandra realizes she would have fared better if she had been told, "I know you feel frustrated when you are not heard. How can you realistically handle this feeling so your frustration won't consume you?" Sandra could not change the past, but she could talk more realistically to herself in the future.

There is a greater motivation to look inward for personal contentment by being realistic about the things another person can or cannot give. While some needs are met through external means, the Christian learns to satisfy neediness through the internal working of the Lord.

LIFESTYLE FACTORS RELATED TO NEEDINESS

Sometimes the neediness of an unfaithful spouse has little to do with childhood deficiencies. Rather, it is an outpouring of undesirable variables in the adult world.

An Inattentive Spouse

It is normal to desire a spouse's affection and expect that marriage will be a place of personal reinforcement where encouragement is given and personal feelings can be shared without fear. But a large percentage of marriages do not provide fulfillment in these personal needs—one or both spouses feel very lonely and unloved. Potential scenarios of an inattentive pattern include:

- A husband assumes his wife should be satisfied as his personal maid and makes no effort to assist in household drudgeries.

- A wife is so preoccupied by the children's activities that she expends little effort in learning about her husband's world.
- A spouse is so engrossed in TV that time is not spent communicating about personal matters.
- Financial problems create preoccupations, which sabotage friendly moments of sharing.
- Church activities supersede family time. The same could be said of job commitments.
- A mate is exceptionally critical, thus inhibiting the growth of love.
- One spouse says, "It's not my habit to open up" and thus excuses himself or herself from becoming involved or vulnerable.

When there is a lack of healthy interaction from one spouse, the other spouse feels a craving to find someone who can share personal issues. Usually efforts are made to force the inattentive spouse to realize the inappropriateness of his or her ways, but the pleas are met with defensiveness and anger. Tension grows and moodiness increases. Obsessive thinking patterns escalate, focusing on the unfairness of the mate's insensitivities. "If only" wishes persist. As the craving for affection grows, the individual loses sight of the possibility of finding inner peace via personal, spiritual avenues. Eventually the shunned spouse feels as if corrective changes will never occur and consciously or unconsciously makes a decision to seek fulfillment elsewhere.

I asked a therapy group of spouses with inattentive mates to share how they handled their neediness so that they would not become vulnerable to rebellious or immoral actions.

"I used to think it was all my fault when my husband was so insensitive. I would cry and wonder what I should do differently to make him happy. The more I did this, the more insecure and lonely I felt. It finally dawned on me that he would be this way no matter what I did. So I determined to no longer browbeat myself. Rather than cater to his every whim, I lived as responsibly as I knew how, and I quit obsessing about his frustrations. He didn't change significantly, but I quit feeling so lowly."

"My response has been to maintain a network of good Christian friends. And I don't just use them as sounding boards to gripe about my marriage. We genuinely enjoy each other's company, and the fellowship partially fills the void that my marriage creates."

"I've learned to look for the positive qualities my wife possesses and comment on them. She is very distant much of the time and hard to reach, but as I focus on the things that are good, my feeling of emptiness is less severe for that moment."

An Overloaded Schedule

Men and women spend years chasing success, jamming their schedules with projects and goals all in the name of getting ahead. In doing so they build huge deficits in the fulfillment of legitimate needs.

Chuck Swindoll put his finger right on target when he described the way people overload their schedules with excessive striving: "In our work-worshipping world, learning to enjoy life is no small task. Many have cultivated such an unrealistic standard of high level achievement that a neurotic compulsion to perform, to compete, to produce, to accomplish the maximum has taken control of our lives."[1] He's right.

What happens to these persons when they finally get fed up with such overload? The healthy ones pare down their schedules and give highest priorities to the activities that really matter, including activities of rest and family enjoyment. The unhealthy ones begin looking for ways to completely abandon the system altogether, even if it means seeking self-serving activities that had previously been considered taboo. Many of these people become involved in an affair hoping that the long overdue need for self-gratification can be found in sensual delight. Implicit in such a decision is a presumed inability to find personal peace through normal channels such as family interactions and solitary moments of meditation with God.

Kent, the minister, told me that for a while he had worked fourteen hours a day including weekends. While his pastoral duties were indeed demanding, he admitted that he easily could have delegated many of them. Instead he prided himself in being the worker no one else could out-perform.

A predictable by-product of this busy life was distance from his wife. When he was at home he had little time or energy to rewardingly share love. By his late thirties he began tiring of work, realizing it could not meet all his personal needs, but by this time he and his wife were so isolated that they had little motivation to try to make their marriage work. Craving intimacy that had been missing for years, he succumbed to the affair, which led to the end of his ministry. Kent had been correct to adjust his schedule to make room for relationship needs, but he sought the wrong means to remove his emptiness.

Persons with schedule overload can do several things to keep it from creating too deep of a hole of neediness: (1) They can recognize that successful life is not measured by busyness or achievement and resolve to become more attuned to the personal side of life; (2) They can put time boundaries on their schedules and stick to them; (3) Leisure time with the family can be scheduled as can time to share personal concerns; (4) Quiet moments of meditation can be set aside each day for prayer and devotion; (5) Duties can be delegated or deleted in order to give family time higher priority.

Recent Failure

Many people have a subconscious need to compensate for the deficits in life. The smallest events can trigger this response. For instance, when a friend tells of an unexpected pay raise we can immediately feel envy as we try to figure how to get our own raise. Or a neighbor tells a funny story involving her son, and we want to at least match that story with a similar anecdote. Or perhaps the spouse points out a flaw which only draws a retaliatory response about one of his or her bad traits. Competition and the possibility of unflattering comparisons quickly bring out insecurity, prompting an effort to make ourselves feel less inadequate.

One precedent to adultery may be a feeling of failure which cannot be put to rest until some success can be claimed. The neediness is shown in that the individual is searching for someone who must say, "I still think you're okay." A person with a recently shattered ego is an easy target for immorality since it seductively offers a quick fix for a deep hurt.

One such case involved Bill. Early in his professional life he had been known as a "wonder boy" who would go straight to the top. Right on schedule he climbed the rungs of the ladder to success, drawing rave reviews along the way. He became known as the one who could always be counted on to deliver. At church he had a similar reputation. He was intelligent and impressed fellow churchgoers with his knowledge of the Bible and church history. On several occasions the church staff asked Bill to assist in particularly delicate matters, and sure enough he came through. But then the unexpected came. Caught making some questionable decisions related to his work, he was asked to resign. His subsequent job was not nearly as rewarding. News about the chink in Bill's armor spread among his friends. In embarrassment he withdrew into a much lower profile. He shunned his wife's attempts to reassure him and within six months it was learned that he had been taking a disreputable woman out for unusually long lunch breaks. No one could understand why such a respected man would so quickly turn away from his prior lifestyle. Bill privately admitted feeling so worthless that he had to have the reassurance of someone who knew nothing about his prior good status.

Often performers think they have inner peace when in fact it is a false smugness based on public approval. They fail to recognize their dependence on praise and status. Such a neediness may go unnoticed until public approval is painfully snatched away, forcing them to draw upon whatever inner strength may or may not be there.

To offset the neediness exposed by failures, one can "plan" to manifest certain traits in specific situations. For example, Bill first had to determine that the empowerment of the Lord was not just a nice-sounding theory, but something real. Bill trained himself to anticipate moments when family members might be less than supportive, then he would consciously commit each circumstance to God, specifically planning to let His patience, confidence, or kindness be in him. This showed Bill that he was capable of internal security in spite of less-than-desirable circumstances. He developed a mental approach to life that was less concerned with achievement and more concerned with yielding to God.

The person who learns to anticipate how planned success can be used in frustrating moments can be transformed from a reactor to an initiator. Emotions will still be influenced by circumstances, but they will not be controlled by them. This clears the way to supplement feelings of neediness with an internally based confidence.

6

Self-Preoccupation

Almost sixteen centuries ago Augustine wrote, "People who are given to pleasing themselves show their emptiness."[1] He concluded, "The highest good in life is to know God and to become completely submersed in the desire to please Him." At the same time he determined that the trait which detracted most from the commitment to life for God was sinful pride, the pre-occupation with one's own cravings.

What makes the words of Augustine stand out is the fact that he was not just writing abstract theory. He was sharing from the heart. Born in northern Africa in A.D. 354, Aurelius Augustinius was the son of a passive father who was a municipal administrator for the Roman government and a strong-willed mother whose sternness created deep bitterness within her son. Possessing a rebellious nature, Augustine was the epitome of "trouble looking for a place to happen" during his teen years. Sexual curiosities dominated his thoughts. Losing his virginity at sixteen, he became a promiscuous rebel. Later he admitted that he had enjoyed sin solely for sin's sake.

As a young adult Augustine shared a live-in relationship with a woman who later bore his son. Eventually his self-seeking ways superseded his sense of responsibility; he abandoned them both and struck out to find himself. He attempted to satisfy his hunger for knowledge by studying the philosophers and dabbling in astrology, but found emptiness. None of his musings satisfied his yearning to understand the conflicts between good and evil. Augustine described these years by writing: "I was led astray myself and I led others astray, deceived and deceiving in all manner of lusts."[2]

Not until he was into his mid-thirties did Augustine begin to understand Christianity and its implications for his lifestyle. Even after his conversion and baptism Augustine remained tormented by his difficulty to find balance in his Christian walk. Finally, through the encouragement of dear friends, he learned the key to contented living: Resist self and let God be God of all. In a prayer of praise he wrote, "This is the blessed life, to rejoice in You, to You, on account of You, this and nothing else. Those who think it other than this pursue another joy which is not true joy."[3]

Augustine's insights can be extremely pertinent to those seeking to understand why they succumbed to promiscuous behavior. They can conclude that the ultimate source of their behavior is a mind fixed on self's desires rather than God's guidance. In counseling, I help these people acknowledge this so they can explore and understand their own impulses.

WHY SELF-PREOCCUPATION OCCURS

Each person who has chosen promiscuity as a form of self-expression admits to many recurring thoughts about personal needs. Such thoughts become so powerful that individuals step across the line of normal self-preservation into the world of self-absorption.

A mind-set focused on selfish cravings is common among those who commit adultery. Many cloak their stories with pleasant-sounding explanations about a love for the third party, but there is still a "what's-in-it-for-me" attitude beneath it all.

For example, Rhonda was a very quiet, reserved woman, conservatively dressed. She would not be considered loose by most people's standards. Her marital frustrations had built for twenty-five years and she was consumed with a craving for relief. When I asked her to tell me about her situation she spoke in calculated tones, "I was getting very tired of waiting for my husband to show affection. He expected me to cater to his every whim yet he seldom showed attention to my needs. I decided it was time to think about myself for a change; that's when the affair began."

"What has happened to you since this all started?"

"Well, I should have seen it coming, but I've been in a state of constant turmoil for the past six weeks. This kind of behavior is unusual for me."

Speaking gently, I responded, "You've probably had moments of depression and anxiety, and I imagine at times you wonder how you got caught in the middle of all this."

"That's an understatement! I knew I was unhappy and I thought this new man could provide me with the excitement I've missed for so many years. In some ways he has. But having an affair is not the romantic high I expected."

"Your weariness with your marital deficiencies is understandable, but it seems that by pursuing this option you've only succeeded in putting yourself under duress."

"You're right. I've never been so high and so low at the same time. Now my life is complicated in ways I never dreamed possible. I don't know why I let my selfishness win."

Why does self-absorption occur? Helping patients realize

several tendencies of human nature provides an answer to this question.

The Natural Inclination Toward Sin

From the beginning God intended for humans to live in freedom, which was balanced by submission to Him. He clearly stated that Adam and Eve had no right to live in full self-control when He instructed them, "Of the tree of the knowledge of good and evil you shall not eat" (Gen. 2:17). Being the Creator of all and the arbitrator of right and wrong, He alone was equipped to properly rule a human's heart and mind. When Satan enticed Eve and then Adam, to eat of the tree and thus "be as God" he succeeded in instilling in them a sense of extreme self-preoccupation. They became self-focused rather than God-focused. They chose to live in self-determination instead of letting God determine the course for living.

No person needs training in this trait. It is inborn. This explains why small children are unwilling to be cooperative. It is indwelling sin that causes such behavior. The same is true for older children, adolescents, and adults. Along the way each person receives "lessons" in selfishness. It is an undeniable feature of human nature. No one is immune from it.

Sexuality represents the peak experience of love. The need for love is so indigenous to each person that it is only natural for both men and women to struggle with selfish love desires. Those claiming to live with no lust delude themselves. Jesus told a group of religiously minded people (the Pharisees) that they could not state that they had never committed adultery. He said, "Whoever looks at a woman to lust for her has already committed adultery with her in his heart" (Matt. 5:28).

Rhonda and I discussed how infidelity was linked to her sin nature. "Rhonda, it is only partially correct to say that your struggles are due to the anger and the loneliness instilled in you by your spouse. To get to the heart of the problem you must recognize that it is part of a spiritual struggle with God regarding the issue of control."

"I've been to church all my life but never quite understood how my personal life is tied to spirituality."

"The most basic question to ask is: 'Who is in charge of my life, me with my wants and desires, or God?'"

The purpose of labeling self-preoccupation as a spiritual matter is to emphasize personal responsibility and accountability to God. King David expressed this when he admitted his adultery with Bathsheba: "Against You, You only, have I sinned" (Ps. 51:4). Any violation against a spouse is a violation against the spouse's Creator.

Heavy Emphasis on Performance

From the early years of childhood each person is required to maintain some standard of performance. During school years the requirement to pass or excel leads us to believe that success is measured by achievements. The adult years perpetuate this pressure with measurements other than grades—salary, titles, social standing—to determine whether a person is either "a somebody" or "a nobody." Many of us expend enormous amounts of energy to do all that we can to develop the reputation of one who performs better than most.

Gary was a good example of the performer who almost became completely self-preoccupied. For twenty years he pursued advances in his corporate world. He was described as the ideal worker who could always be counted on to produce. Gary pointed to his family history with great pride recalling the strong work ethic that his father had instilled in him. The philosophy he lived by was "Never let others do what you can do yourself."

At age forty-three, Gary announced to his family that he was moving out because he had found someone new that he wanted to date. He told me, "I have always been able to do what my mind set out to do, and I have never been denied my just rewards. At home I tried being the best husband and father, but I was not given the appreciation I deserved."

I thought a moment and replied, "In other words, you performed your job well at home and the 'pay' was not in your range, so you sought a new arena where the rewards would be more forthcoming."

"That doesn't sound very flattering, but I guess that's one way of saying it."

Gary regularly sought applause or reinforcements so that he began to believe that rewards—overt gratitude—were a must; a good performance by itself was not rewarding enough. Eventually this resulted in an "I deserve the best of everything" mentality, including covert sexual pleasures.

Gary chose not to give up his girlfriend for several months because he considered her to be an earned trophy. Gary represents a performer who was so consumed with self that the payoff superseded responsibility.

It is normal to appreciate positive reinforcement at the end of a solid performance. No human is so altruistic that every deed can be done with no thought of some kind of remuneration. This need may be tempered by a willingness to perform some good works for sheer enjoyment.

A Pattern of Repressed Emotions

Frequently, the unfaithful spouse experiences an additional problem that feeds self-preoccupation: the repression of emotions. Many of these people have lived in an environment that inhibited a healthy exploration of feelings. The result: a pattern of either hiding or avoiding emotions. But repressed emotions do not just disappear; they eventually gain internal strength until they demand almost obsessive attention from the individual.

Perhaps a parent punished the child or took away the child's allowance when he or she cried. The home atmosphere may have been so unstable that the child learned to play it safe and keep feelings bottled up. These kinds of scenarios result in a lifelong habit of holding in feelings. Feelings were rarely shared or satisfactorily resolved.

Gary recalled that if he ever expressed an emotion (usually frustration) he was either sharply told what to do or he was invalidated for what he felt.

"I remember when my mother told me that I had to sing in the boys' choir at church and I told her that I wasn't really interested in music. Mom said that I was silly for saying that and she would hear no more of such nonsense," Gary told me.

"So you exposed a preference and immediately your feeling was walked on."

"I just wanted her to understand how I felt. I would have done what she asked, but it was humiliating to feel that I couldn't even state how I felt."

"What did you do whenever you had something personal to share after that experience?"

"I kept it inside."

"Did those feelings just disappear?"

"Oh no! If anything, I developed a stronger urge to have things my way."

This is natural; emotions do not just disappear when they are repressed. They eventually gain an internal strength and demand almost obsessive attention from the individual. Predictably, Gary carried this habit into his marriage. He told his wife she was weak if she cried or expressed insecurity. He avoided conversations that involved touchy subjects. He rebuked his children for being too emotional.

Gary's wife was quite surprised to learn what attracted him

to the other woman: "She was someone I could share personal things with." Gary finally concluded that life could be much more rewarding if he openly shared the deepest parts of himself. Unfortunately he assumed that the pattern of emotional repression could not be remedied within his marriage so he made the mistake of drawing another woman into his confidences.

Gary's self-preoccupation could have been prevented if he had learned to express and contemplate his emotions as a child.

A Habit of Having It My Way

In one session Rhonda, in her typical cautious voice, told me that the most difficult aspect of her life was meeting the needs of her husband and children. During counseling she realized that as a child she had grown accustomed to attending almost solely to her own social needs, without worrying too much about anyone else's concerns. She admitted that perhaps she was spoiled, which also hindered her ability to be content as a servant. Until then she had never really considered herself a self-centered person.

"Rhonda, to most people you seem so cooperative. It would surprise many to learn that you have this self-oriented way of thinking."

Smiling as if she had been caught, she responded, "Oh, I always learned to play the game of being socially appropriate. But I knew that if I kept a good reputation, most things would turn out the way I wanted."

"Do you remember consciously thinking this way about your marriage?"

"Sure. My parents catered to me because I was always a good kid, so why wouldn't my husband do the same? It finally dawned on me after years of giving in to him that he would never treat me the way I assumed he should. That's when I decided to let loose."

Most developing children are not naturally inclined to think more about the needs of others than about themselves. Some parents successfully train their children to be genuinely considerate and giving, yet the norm leans more toward expending energy for selfish purposes. This quality is not unique to the young. Adults maintain many of the same traits, only with more sophistication.

Our culture strongly encourages egocentricity. In matters of grooming, professional striving, or pleasure seeking, we are trained to do all we can to get what is best for ourselves. Some of this striving is reasonable, but it becomes a troublesome habit when it feeds the desire for privileged status.

For example, many of us attempt to create a home atmosphere suited for most of our desires. A man may have definite ideas about the amount of starch in his shirts and becomes critical or temperamental when his preferences are not met. A wife may expect cooperation in household chores. When these matters go unattended, she becomes annoyed and resentful.

"I tried telling my husband and children how they could help me," Rhonda said, "but they never took me seriously. So I just did what I had to do!"

"What other options of self-preservation had you considered?" I asked, trying to show Rhonda that there were other solutions to her problem.

"I know I should have been more tolerant and expressed my frustrations more lovingly and openly, but I was tired of talking with them and then meeting resistance."

I had no desire to convince Rhonda that it was always wrong to look out for personal needs. Jesus Himself was described as taking moments to get away from some of His daily pressures.

113

My goal was to help her find balance between selfishness and responsibility so morality could be maintained.

A Lack of Deep Meaning in Life

One of the most flippant men that I have talked with shrugged as he rationalized his many adulteries: "Hey, you only go around once so you have to get all that you can." His mischievous laugh indicated that he did not consider life a serious matter—he could do whatever he desired without worrying about old-fashioned guilt. I suspected that this man rarely contemplated why God had given him life or the depth of love that could be experienced in an exclusive union with his wife.

Most unfaithful spouses are not as blatantly shallow as this man, but they experience confusion regarding the real meaning of life during the time of the adultery. Interestingly, some of these people are capable of reciting from rote memory the "correct" answers to questions regarding their purpose before God: "to serve God and to love others." Yet they claim that Christianity doesn't have the same appeal it once had. Others complain that a habit of family devotion is too cumbersome and not as rewarding as it should be. They enter a state of identity confusion, and with few deep roots they justify a lifestyle bent on pleasing self.

One of the most clearly documented struggles for meaning in life is recorded in the book of Ecclesiastes. Though possessing an intellect second to no one, Solomon had a period of time when he was not sufficiently grounded in God in a way that led to a sense of purpose. Consequently he was easily pulled into a lifestyle of wine, women, and song. Solomon wrote, "Whatever my eyes desired I did not keep from them. I did not withhold my heart from any pleasure" (Eccles. 2:10). Eventually he concluded that such self-seeking was vanity. He admitted that his life would know little more than empty selfishness as long as his meaning was not grounded in God. "For in the multitude of dreams and many words there is also vanity. But, fear God" (Eccles. 5:7).

When life is not rooted in a meaningful relationship with God, the guiding philosophy tends to be "My life belongs to myself." Then men and women are doomed to the philosophy of humanism. They may continue to perform some pleasant acts of kindness and may be quite friendly and giving in relationships, but they are susceptible to falling into the natural selfish habits that persistently tempt humans.

BREAKING THE HOLD OF SELF-PREOCCUPATION

Once the habit of self-preoccupation is identified and understood, unfaithful spouses can experience tremendous growth. I walk my patients through several steps leading to that end.

Step #1: Filter Your Behaviors Through a Commitment to Christ.

In counseling Rhonda, I sensed that she wanted to make Christianity real in her life, as it had been many years before. So I said: "Rhonda, I know you are unhappy with the way your life has unfolded. You never expected to be in this predicament."

"I would like to return to a Christian way of life, but I don't know how. It's all been so theoretical to me."

"Let's focus on two words: *control* and *choice*. Your first task is to determine who is in control of your life: your husband, another man, your boss, or God. Your second task is to realize that you can choose to be ruled by whatever makes the most sense to you."

Then we discussed Galatians 2:20: "I have been crucified

with Christ; it is no longer I who live, but Christ lives in me." We noted how this entailed a choice to lay self's preoccupations aside and allow Christ to control her will. This meant that when she had a moral decision to make she would yield her preference to God's. When she asked her family to help her with household tasks, she could speak with the Lord's kindness rather than with her own impatience. When she acted as a servant it would be done with a spirit of willingness rather than duty.

"Rhonda, this is not something you *have to* do. It is a choice. You can remain preoccupied with your own desires and hold the controls yourself, or you can give control to God.

"The apostle Paul told the Colossians that the person who has set his or her mind on God's ways will have a life 'hidden in Christ.' That person is cloaked by Christ's ways as ideas are yielded to Him. Behaviors are guided by Him. As Christians we are to be so identified with Christ that we lose selfish desires.

"You won't be perfect in giving God the controls, but you can develop a habit of living in Christ's ways."

People have told me countless times that they became most vulnerable to an affair when they ceased in their devotion to God or when Christianity became so routine that it had little depth. Without the conscious awareness of a yieldedness to God, Satan gained a foothold and tempted these persons to return to self-centered living. James 4:7–8 promises, "Therefore submit to God. Resist the devil and he will flee from you. Draw near to God and He will draw near to you."

Those wishing to conquer self-preoccupation which leads to adultery do best when involved in regular devotion time and Bible study—some with a group and some alone. Every effort should be made to separate from persons who deride God's ways. Lifestyle adjustments to shun worldly entertainment should also be made. Salvation will become the dearest personal possession of all.

Step #2: Recognize the Universality of Your Struggles.

When the temptation to commit adultery is at its peak, men and women often experience tunnel vision regarding personal desires; they feel as if they are the only ones suffering a frustrated life: "Oh sure, others have their problems, too, but they are not quite like *my* problems." Armed with the notion that the difficulties in other marriages are somehow less painful than their own problems, they begin the process of rationalization.

Rhonda once told me, "When I sit in church I observe the way other families appear and they seem so pleasant and comfortable. Then I think about the chronic friction in our home and before you know it I feel angry and cheated." Her lament is shared by many. But her comparisons are based on very superficial impressions, so her conclusions are probably inaccurate.

Even families enjoying genuine camaraderie and love have tensions. They determine to rise above their problems. In actuality these ideal situations represent a minority of cases. The high divorce rate indicates that many are struggling with unhappiness (conservative estimates suggest that one in three marriages will end in divorce). Other couples may not divorce but will stick it out, gritting their teeth the entire way.

Spouses wanting to find an excuse to nurse self-preoccupied complaints will have no trouble doing so. Yet honesty requires that they acknowledge they are not unique in their troubles.

When this fact is accepted it will influence other thoughts. The individual will realize that a privileged status cannot be rightfully claimed. Self will not be considered as the center of the universe. A sense of community can be felt with others who also experience ups and downs.

Step #3: Submission Will Be a Part of One's Life.

I recall the look on Gary's face when I suggested that a characteristic that would be instrumental in his personal growth was submission. One eyebrow shot up as a look of confusion fell over him: "No man is supposed to be submissive! I may sound old-fashioned, but that's reserved for a woman. A man should be the leader."

An unfortunate thing has happened to the beliefs of some Christians. Many have construed submission to be strictly a feminine word. Based on the instructions in Ephesians 5:22 and in 1 Peter 3:1, women have been told that they are supposed to live under the rule of their husbands. Some follow such instruction with quiet compliance. Others rebel wildly.

Two errors may result from such teaching. The first is that wives can be duped into believing that submission requires a lack of opinions or decisiveness. The second is that men can overlook the fact that they are also taught to live in subjection to their wives (Eph. 5:21). Submission is not a feminine word or a mandate to live in such a weakened state that others are allowed to be condescending.

Submission is defined as living in a mission for God. Intended for both males and females, it is the embodiment of a loving disposition that reveals God's grace to others. When persons choose to live in submission they return to the first instruction given to humanity: "Of every tree of the garden you may freely eat; but of the tree of the knowledge of good and evil you shall not eat (Gen. 2:17). Submissive people understand that God's original blueprint for living called for a commitment to live under His authority, learn His ways, and follow His instructions. In fact, one lesson taught by Jesus Christ was to always acquiesce to the Father's will even if it meant setting aside our own preferences.

Jesus honestly revealed His dread of the Cross in the Garden of Gethsemane when He expressed His emotions but then prayed, "Not my will, but Thine be done."

I told Gary some of these thoughts during our counseling session. Then I said, "I agree that a man is to lead his wife. This is accomplished by setting the pace in servitude. Gary, you'll find more rewards by lifting your wife to a position of honor, even if sometimes you have to accept lowliness. When you are submissive by looking out for her needs, your influence with her will increase."

God has given men the responsibility of valuing their wives and building security in their children, even if the effort is not reciprocated. Wives can consider it their role to maintain harmony at home, avoiding a critical spirit but willing to encourage and stimulate.

Step #4: Be an Imitator of God.

Remember how children learn to write? I recall my daughter's excitement as she was learning to put her ABCs on paper. The method of teaching her was simple. As her parents we would print a letter then hand the pencil to her with the instruction, "Now you do what we just did." Sometimes the process of learning seemed painstakingly slow, yet modeling was the only way to get the job done.

The biblical instruction to "be imitators of God, as beloved children" reflects this modeling process. Just as a young child learns by watching the more masterful authority, we are taught to assume the childlike position of observing, then modeling God.

In Old Testament days God was considered by most to be a distant, almost unapproachable authority figure, but Jesus introduced the idea that we could relate to God in very personal terms. He told us to call God by a new name, not the Old Testament name of *Yahweh* ("I am") or *Adonai* (Lord), but *Father*. Jesus brought the incredible news that while we should still hold God in reverential awe, we are also allowed to consider ourselves as His children. When we become Christians, we are commissioned to represent Him to family, friends, and acquaintances.

Gary was not quick to let go of the personality traits that underlaid his infidelity. His turning point came as a result of a study he made regarding the attributes of God: holiness, justice, sovereignty, and wisdom. "I was reminded," he said, "that there is a being much grander than me." Gary also recognized God's mercy and grace, which propelled God to provide eternal salvation for all who would receive it.

"Les, until recently my inclination has been to live for me because I assumed that I should receive whatever I said I deserve. But I have been forced to realize that there is more to life than just me, and I don't have the right to call all the shots. Only God does.

"I'm committed to letting God be God, and my desire is to reflect His ways in my lifestyle. This is going to be a real change for me." He determined to acknowledge his own childish state, guided by selfish desires, then to daily appeal to God to show him the way to successful living.

By being imitators of God we can train ourselves to pause when self-preoccupied urges appear and ask, "Father, what would You have me be at this moment?" This acquiescence is not natural to human nature, but it can be practiced often enough to become an established habit.

In the next chapter, the craving for freedom, another major element undergirding marital infidelity, is examined.

7

The Craving for Unbridled Freedom

Lynette, with a slightly stocky build, seemed to possess a strong personality which would take second place to no one. Friendly, even jovial, it was clear that she enjoyed being center stage. She spoke in confident tones, yet I detected that beneath the veneer was an insecure woman, frustrated with her inability to understand her own emotions and behaviors.

"Gene and I met in college when we each had part-time jobs at the same place. He was always very courteous and would escort me to my car each night. He was always a true gentleman. When we began dating he was very mannerly and wouldn't hear of anyone speaking poorly of me. I was really flattered. I noticed that he was a little overprotective, but that's what I liked most about him.

"I was totally unprepared, though, for the extreme possessiveness Gene showed after we married. After the honeymoon I began feeling less flattered and more annoyed by his protectiveness. It seemed that he didn't give me credit for any ability to think. He was always telling me where I should go, when I should go, who I could go with, and how I should act. When I told him to ease up, he seemed offended. He really didn't understand me."

Gene's need to be in control brought increasing frustration as each year of marriage passed. Lynette had to account for every dollar she spent. Gene set a routine that he expected her to follow when they came home each evening. If she had a preference different from his, she was told to cooperate with his leadership. She was accused of being argumentative if she expressed a strong opinion. She explained, "I'm not exactly an overly dependent person and I really resent his control."

Lynette was an example of a person who felt so overwhelmed by her mate that she determined to break his hold, even if it meant giving herself to another man.

After storing up resentment and frustration for twelve years, Lynette met a man at her part-time job who seemed to be Gene's opposite. Whereas her husband was stubborn, bossy, and suspicious, he was flexible, solicitous, and trusting. She told me, "I didn't fully realize how emotionally exhausted I had become in the wake of Gene's controlling ways. I was so taken by this man's relaxed attitude that I felt magnetically attracted to him."

I have heard countless similar recollections. The desire to leave home grows when restrictive, picky rules are imposed. Frequently these impositions are technically correct, yet burdensome to relational growth.

For example, Lynette's husband wanted a clean house and would gripe until she got it clean. Gene wanted her to be pleasant to their children at all times and would correct Lynette if she was edgy. He was a very precise communicator, so he insisted that she speak with crisp clarity. He was quite imposing in his desires, but none of these preferences could be considered abnormal. Gene pressed on thinking he was correct. If his orders were not fulfilled, punishment followed. Control tactics were employed repetitively. They only inflamed the atmosphere of frustration, but they were continued. Why? Because correctness had to be preserved. In the meantime, love was lost.

Whenever I meet with a couple together, or with either spouse alone, I always help them uncover the dynamics of their relationship. Invariably both faithful and unfaithful spouses need to consider changes before the marriage relationship can be restored. This is particularly true when control and criticism are involved.

THE HIDDEN MESSAGES OF CONTROL

When control becomes a part of the home atmosphere, a silent but powerful system of underground communication is perpetuated. It instills a desire to flee within the controlled mate. To understand the dynamics of adultery more clearly, couples must identify the hidden communications that accompany a controlling home environment.

"Fit My Mold"

Many unfaithful spouses complain of a home atmosphere so full of expectations that it is impossible to remember the next "supposed to," much less live correctly. These duties are often spoken in the form of criticisms, commands, or strong suggestions. They may be adaptations of biblical instructions or family traditions that cannot and will not be laid to rest.

For example, Jerry was dragged to my office by his wife, Susan, who had caught him in an affair. When I asked them to tell me of their home environment, he was quick to mention that his wife had had a very definite agenda for him to fulfill since the first day of their marriage. He explained that she expected him to handle himself in very specific ways socially. She corrected him on how he should speak, told him what to wear, and had to approve of his buddies.

Likewise, she expected him to be a model husband and father. He had to spend time with the children, exhibit all Christian attributes, and care for her aging father.

When in social circles, she would remind him of proper etiquette, off-limits topics of conversation, and proper ways to address the ladies. Jerry threw up his hands and complained, "She had my whole life planned for me—how I look, what I say, and how I should feel. I couldn't take it anymore." Susan listened to these complaints with a look of incredulity on her face, as if Jerry were describing another person. "If you can show me that I'm wrong, I'll stop making suggestions," she said. "But everything I say to you is for your own good."

Jerry quickly responded, "I didn't marry you so you could be my mother! Even my own mother was easier to live with than you. I *hate* being told what to do!"

Susan looked toward me and sighed, "How can I respect a word he says when he shouts like this?" She seemed oblivious to the fact that she was attempting to keep him in a fence. She had not learned the balance between being principled and being loving. As a result, Jerry's craving to be shed of her mold was so great that he was blinded to morality.

It is necessary to live with firm values in this age that shuns absolutes, but it is inappropriate for one person to impose an absolute mold upon another. This is particularly true in a marriage since expectations can easily feed power struggles.

Scripture teaches Christians to exhort, instruct, and stimulate one another. There is strength when two work jointly toward building character. But nowhere does Scripture give one individual the right to coerce another into a mold. The biblical concept of the priesthood of believers conveys each individual's freedom to determine how to interpret God's will. We should be humble enough to listen to others' suggestions, but we each have the prerogative to choose our own molds.

"Conform to My Rules for Rules' Sake"

This statement is a second cousin to "fit my mold." However, in this case the controller is an institution or a representative (parents, pastors, church elders, or community).

Conformity to rules for conformity's sake begins in childhood and continues throughout adulthood. Many homes, schools, and churches teach moral principles but when the child asks "Why?" the answer is: "Because that's the way it's supposed to be." The child is given little room for contemplative thinking as he or she learns, "I'd better live right whether I like it or not."

As these children become adults they continue to appear to agree with traditional norms even though they feel disposed to live otherwise. They have learned to deceive themselves and others by saying all the "right" things in order to live and be accepted.

Lynette expressed this dilemma by saying, "I grew up in a very conservative fundamentalist church environment. When we were told the difference between right and wrong, there was no questioning. I felt compelled to marry a man of unwavering principle, and after marriage I stayed within the circle of people who believed as I had been taught. As each year passed I liked their rules less and less. I guess I fooled everybody by appearing to go along with their ways. My affair was a way of stepping out and making a statement they couldn't ignore."

"Lynette, does this mean you have rejected your earlier beliefs?"

"No, it doesn't," she replied with a loud sigh. "If anything, I respect those principles more. I've seen firsthand what life is like without them."

Rules that are imposed dogmatically tend to lose their effect on individuals. The intellect may still endorse the rules, but the emotions cry for freedom. Such legalism becomes a trap that individuals wish to escape, much like the feeling an energetic boy has when forced to sit quietly with his hands folded while adults talk in Grandma's living room.

"You Are Not Acceptable"

The words "You are not acceptable" may never be openly expressed, but persistent control communicates limited and conditional acceptance. A stringent standard is held before the accused who is expected to explain why the standard is not adequately met. The rejection may not be directly verbalized, but it is implied by persistent criticism, dogmatic stubbornness, a fretting disposition, and inflexible attitudes like Gene's.

Gene looked genuinely stunned when Lynette insisted that she did not feel accepted by him. He rambled on about the many sacrifices he had made on her behalf as proof of his love. Her retort was that he demanded so much and criticized her so frequently that she did not believe him when he expressed any positive regard.

"But Lynette, won't you admit that I have been a perfect gentleman since we first met? Doesn't that tell you something?"

"Yes, it tells me that you are a prim and proper person. At first I thought of it as love. But now I only interpret it as meaning that I'm not good enough for you."

"Well, what more can I do to make you feel accepted? I'm not sure I understand."

"Why don't you start by easing up on your perfectionism? If

you could be casual and smile more often I would feel ten times more relaxed with you."

Acceptance can be communicated in a myriad of ways. Overtly it can be expressed through such affirmative words as, "I love you" or "I'm glad that you and I are friends." Covertly it can be communicated with a gentle smile, a touch, or a listening ear. Virtually every person has subconscious sensors detecting when an atmosphere of acceptance is or is not present.

Genuine acceptance means that preconditions are not required before love or respect is offered. No agenda accompanies acceptance; this allows people to be what they are. Husbands and wives can still offer principles and opinions, sometimes with consequences, yet they do not ram them at their spouses or suggest punitive intentions.

"I Don't Trust You"

Control implies untrustworthiness. When a lack of trust is ever present it tends to become a self-fulfilling prophecy. I witness a recurring scenario of spouses who question each other's feelings, ideas, and perceptions so often that marital dissatisfaction grows with each resulting quarrel. Lynette told me: "I'm tired of trying to appease Gene after all these years." She then reminded Gene of conversations when she had to justify her parenting skills, her daily schedule, her feelings of support for him, and her spending practices.

"One example stands out in my mind," she said. "We were coming home from church recently when you chided me for telling a friend that I had been to the doctor that week to take care of an infection. You told me that it was improper to discuss personal matters like that because only family should know of such concerns. I felt like a six-year-old whose judgment was suspect. It was as though I had no ability to think or act intelligently. I hate being anywhere with you because I feel so scrutinized." Since Lynette was not considered trustworthy, her behavior eventually reflected the expectation.

Demonstrating trust within marriage has potential risks—there is the possibility that the spouse will act in less-than-desirable ways. I have heard dictatorial spouses like Gene complain, "If I let my mate go free, I'll live to regret it." They attempt to live with vigilance, marking every move the spouse makes. This never produces satisfactory feelings since a suspicious mind is unable to find the best in others.

Offering trust may be risky, particularly toward a partner susceptible to infidelity, but it is better than excessive control. The gift of trust can be a boost to the mate's security, as well as a tonic for one's personal well-being. If the trust is broken, measures can be taken to impose consequences. But if trust is never given, it is virtually guaranteed that trustworthiness will never grow.

"I'm Superior to You"

Superiority is another message that accompanies a controlling atmosphere. The mate who dogmatically sets the parameters assumes a posture of authority, relegating the other into coerced subservience. The Bible teaches the benefits of a husband's authority (leadership) in the home, but this trait should not be construed as a license to dominate. Authority is to be grounded in humility and love.

Many times the messages of superiority are subtle. For example, some spouses may never be overtly bossy or dictatorial, but they may be constant nitpickers. Perhaps a mate will not directly prohibit the other from an activity, but the propensity toward worry and fretting may be so overwhelming that control is undeniable. Or the controlling spouse may use the silent treatment to show displeasure. Each of these actions expresses a condescending assumption that the mate's ways are not as important or valid.

Jerry, the husband who was dragged into counseling by his wife, quickly agreed that in his wife's mind he was inferior to her. He told me, "I felt as if she was the queen and I was the serf. When I would suggest how to handle a problem with our son, she usually explained why my suggestion would not work. Once I wore a suit to dinner that she didn't like so she didn't speak to me for the next two days."

Sensing defeat in his voice, I asked, "How do you normally respond to this message of superiority?"

"Earlier in our marriage I would argue back, but she is so stubborn, much more so than I. She knew I would eventually relent, and she would 'prove' that she was more powerful. Finally I just kept my mouth shut."

"How do you relate this to the affair?"

"That question is easy to answer. I would regularly run into the other woman at work and always detected a respect for me. Not once did she look down her nose at me. Not once did she act like a boss toward me. She just met me at my level. It was so refreshing I couldn't resist her.

"At first I began finding excuses to be around her. I had no plans of letting it turn into anything serious. But you're vulnerable when you've been spoken down to so often."

Jerry's struggle with inferiority predated his days with his wife. He fought feelings of defeat in his youth; he had to struggle to keep up scholastically and athletically with his peers. Then he married Susan, who came from a family of very successful businessmen. He felt like he was constantly in their shadow. He could not blame these circumstances for his affair, but they created a craving to be on equal ground with another person.

BALANCED FREEDOM

If I stood on a street corner and asked the first one hundred passersby whether they would rather live in America or the USSR, the responses would probably be unanimous. If each was asked to specify the reason for preferring America, the answer would be consistent: "Here, we have freedom."

Deep within the heart of each human is an undeniable desire to be free. But interestingly, not all of the people who celebrate national freedoms are willing to allow freedom in marriage. Instead they vie for control.

Freedom is defined as the presence of choices. Each option is accompanied by a consequence, yet it is a privilege to sift through the various possibilities, weigh the pros and cons, and arrive at conclusions.

Since an unfaithful spouse is seeking freedom from restrictive circumstances, I encourage that person to examine the available options.

1. Sin Is Only One Alternative.

As a parent I remind myself daily that it is not my job to dictate to my daughter, Cara, how she must live. If she is to eventually function as a healthy adult, she must have plenty of practice exercising free will. But concurrently, I am concerned for her well-being, and I am more knowledgeable than she is regarding issues of right and wrong, appropriateness and inappropriateness. I want her to experience freedom, but I also have a set of beliefs to instill in her mind.

My task is to guide her toward my preferred goals while giving her true freedom. I do this by helping her recognize the consequences of her actions. She is free to choose how to live, but she learns that each choice is followed by some type of reinforcement, sometimes pleasurable, sometimes not.

God has the same dilemma as Father to each Christian. He hates sin but wants to preserve mankind's freedom to choose. He also uses the system of consequences to communicate His desires. The consequences are His way of communicating the error of following sinful cravings. As we learn to anticipate the pains that accompany sinful choices, we conclude that sin is freely available, but undesirable.

Each unfaithful person knows that infidelity is a sin. Some are too calloused to contemplate the word *sin,* yet their deceptiveness reveals an intuitive understanding of its wrongness. They are completely free to make such choices. No one can truthfully say, "You cannot commit adultery." When faced with the temptation to be unfaithful, the question to contemplate is not "Can I do it?" but "Will I choose it?"

Lynette pondered the repercussions of her affair. "I knew it was wrong to be with another man from the beginning, but I wanted to get away from Gene's domination so badly that I told myself that I didn't care what might happen."

"In other words, you were so focused on just getting away with the affair that your mind didn't examine the big picture."

"That's right. The worst thing is that my mother now knows the whole story." She paused as tears came to her eyes. "And even though she says she is in my corner it hurts to know that I've hurt her. Now most of my friends know and I feel embarrassed to be with them." Clenching her fists, she spoke with difficulty. "I was desperate to get away from Gene because I was in so much pain, but the affair only increased my misery."

Sin is always an alternative, but never a good one. The perpetrator should brace himself for negative repercussions when he chooses to follow the desires of sin.

2. Reactive Behaviors Imply a Type of Enslavement.

It is true that most unfaithful spouses, like Lynette, are seeking freedom. The irony is that their angry reaction to another's control indicates they are not really free. Lynette may have escaped the fence Gene had built, but she was not truly autonomous. Her behavior was still being driven by her husband.

I have never known a person to say, "I'd really like to be an unfaithful spouse; that sounds like a fine goal." Rather, this choice is a frustrated reaction to the manner in which they have been treated by others; they are rebellious, yet still manipulated by someone else. The apostle Peter warned us that ". . . by whom a person is overcome, by him also he is brought into bondage" (2 Pet. 2:19).

Lynette made a personal breakthrough when she admitted that her childhood was full of frustration because her mother bossed and coerced her into living as a proper young lady. She had married Gene too young, a man who was also very overpowering and strong willed. She developed many infatuations during her marriage, and after twelve years she became sexually involved with another man.

Lynette's insight into the motives that were driving her came when we discussed how she had consistently lived her life in reaction to others with little freedom to think for herself.

"Lynette, during your entire adult life you have had the capability to make free choices, but it seems that you were rarely permitted, either in your childhood or your marriage, to exercise that privilege."

"That sounds so simple, yet you're right," Lynette agreed.

"When you made the decision to become involved in the affair, a choice was involved. But now I'm hearing you state that this choice was not consistent with your deepest beliefs."

"So you are saying that I was still in a type of bondage?"

"Exactly. True freedom means you have the time to think about your guiding beliefs and the clarity of mind to choose to live out what you say you believe."

"Les, I'm not sure I would know how to handle it if I truly had permission to think about my every activity. It would feel strange."

"Yes, it would feel strange. But I would rather have you contemplate your activities with a free mind than to watch you continue to 'steal' your freedom through rebellion."

Genuinely free individuals are initiators. Not satisfied to live in reaction to others, they examine the pros and cons of their behaviors and determine the best course for their lives.

Lynette was free to commit adultery, stay married, or move to Tahiti. She decided to commit to a married life with no sexual distractions. This belief happened to coincide with the instructions of her parents, friends, and the church. The key was that now it was *her* belief.

3. Each Person Can Choose the Course of His Own Emotions.

Personal responsibility is the natural companion to freedom. We cannot always determine which emotions will or will not appear on our mental screens, but we can choose their directions.

I once counseled a man who had spent several years in prison where he was accountable for every aspect of living. He even had to record the number of socks and undergarments kept in his tiny room. Even in such a restrictive atmosphere he learned to exercise choices. He found that he was free to hate or free to accept. He had the option to bear grudges or to forgive. He could correspond with his family or ignore them. He could be pleasant with, scream at, or withdraw from those he encountered daily. His external circumstances were severely restricted, yet he had correctly concluded that the inner world of his emotions was still subject to free choices.

Each person has a wide range of affirmative and negative

emotions from which to choose, even when a job is oppressive, a marriage burdensome, or a social spotlight intense. People can take time to contemplate the variety of possibilities rather than giving prominence to the first reaction that appears. For example, once Lynette decided to commit to marriage, she still had the choice to be aloof, fume in silent anger, or scream as loudly as possible. These choices are unwise, but they are available. Lynette could also choose to accept Gene with no preconditions, to confront him in healthy assertiveness, to forgive, and to live in kindness. All options were open; it was up to Lynette to determine what seemed best.

After spending a Saturday with Gene, Lynette happily shared a personal victory with me: "We almost got caught in one of our old spats. I felt Gene was being too finicky about our daughter's clothes. In the past I would have fumed about how controlling he was, and it would have ruined the whole day."

"What made this time different?"

"My common sense told me that fuming had never worked in the past and wasn't going to do any good now. Fuming was still a choice, but I decided that acceptance was a better choice."

"What about your feelings of entrapment?"

"I didn't feel trapped by him at all. How can I be trapped when I am living with my own choices?"

When we choose our emotional reactions to a situation, life is not a series of quick reflex reactions, but a coherent philosophy. Our emotions can be guided (though not totally vetoed) by thoughtful beliefs and goals.

4. All Other People Are Free to Live As They Choose.

If an individual claims the God-given privilege to live in freedom, it would only be fair to let others choose the course of their lives. The temptation to coerce another person may be powerful when that individual is behaving against our own beliefs, particularly when that person is a close family member. But we fool ourselves when we insist that another person *must* behave in certain ways.

Two examples from Scripture underscore the concept of giving others freedom: the prodigal son (Luke 15:11–24) and the rich young ruler (Matt. 19:16–22). In the first story the father granted freedom to the rebellious son even though he knew that the freedom would be abused. The story has a positive conclusion because the young man's choices caused him to regret his decisions and return to his father's ways. In the other example the rich young ruler asked Jesus the prerequisites for discipleship. He did not like Jesus' reply so he turned and walked away, never to encounter Him again. In each case, the individual was allowed to make a noncoerced decision.

It is the same in healthy marital relationships. All mates are free to act impatiently, rudely, or passively. They can communicate with openness or be defensive. They are free to be supportive or totally disinterested. They can treat family members politely or behave as tyrants. To deny these alternatives is to misunderstand human nature.

Jerry looked back upon the years spent with a wife who spoke condescendingly to him and realized that he had become so incensed with her character that he failed to recognize that she was perfectly free to be as she chose. He told me, "I knew my inward tensions grew as I refused to recognize her freedom to be who she was."

"I see that you've realized that you responded to her regulatory ways with some regulations of your own."

"I hate to admit it, but that's precisely what I've done. I've got to realize that she is free to be exactly who she is. I'm only harming myself and adding to our home tension by wishing she would be something she isn't."

"Do you suppose that recognizing her freedom will mean that you have to lie down and let her walk on you?"

"Not at all. Now I can see that it is possible to express my opinions without getting entangled in a power play."

The gift of freedom does not relegate the giver to a position of wimpiness. Firm convictions can be expressed and moral parameters can be drawn. By offering his wife this kind of freedom, Jerry maintained his own freedom—his emotions would not be directly tied to her behavior.

5. The Bond Slave Attitude Is Ultimate Freedom.

In the days of Roman rule, a master could present his slave with freedom papers. But the individual might choose to remain like a slave, though he and the master knew that he could leave at any time. Similarly a human relationship is elevated to a higher plateau when partners agree that they are not bound together by dogmatic restraints, but by a mutual commitment to maintain a cohesive relationship.

The bond slave's attitude is best applied in relationships anchored in the Lord. Being deeply committed to the guidance of Christ, individuals will know they are capable of choosing wrongful ways, but will have such an intense desire to please God that they will surrender to Him. Paul went so far in describing the mind of a bond servant that he gave us the instruction to consider ourselves dead in order to let Christ live in us: "I have been crucified with Christ; it is no longer I who live, but Christ lives in me" (Gal. 2:20).

The implications within marriage are enormous: a faithful spouse may resent the other, but he or she knows that the Lord prefers kindness, so the spouse yields that resentment. A faithful mate also knows that he or she has biblical grounds for divorce, but before making that decision, the mate devotes time and prayer to determine God's desires. He or she might realize that the unfaithful spouse has a less mature understanding of the Christian life, and therefore he or she decides to encourage the unfaithful spouse toward greater maturity and responsibility.

Understanding the whys of an affair can assist both the unfaithful and the injured spouse to determine adjustments that will lead to a healthier marriage. Yet knowing why an affair occurs is only part of the equation for healing. There also needs to be an examination of the deception that accompanies infidelity. Part 3 identifies the deceptions the unfaithful spouse needs to eliminate before a reconciliation with the faithful spouse can occur.

PART 3

Discerning Fact
from Fiction

8

The Deception
of Others

The lifestyle of adultery may reveal a strange creative genius in people. Tom explains, "I've concocted so many imaginative stories to explain my whereabouts that I amaze myself with my ability to sell lies. I've had so many supposed meetings, emergencies, and unexpected tie-ups that my wife should have figured that my world was too unpredictable to be believed. But until last month my salesmanship got me off the hook time after time."

Sixteen years ago Tom married Ellen. They now have three preteen sons. I asked him to describe his marriage relationship and he told me it was not all bad: "We've had ups and downs through the years, but we don't argue much. We've gone a couple of months or more without even a cross word. Ellen is real devoted to our boys and enjoys being a housewife. We don't talk much, but that's probably been my fault more than hers."

Wanting to get to the heart of their problem, I fished: "I'm assuming by your presence in my office that not all has been well through the years."

"You can say that again. We may go long periods between arguments, but the same can be said about our sex life. We've gone as long as a year without being intimate. Ellen and I exist together but we don't have much companionship."

"When did you begin being less attracted to her and more attracted to another woman?"

"Oh, I don't know. Maybe a year or two ago. I got tired of being rebuffed sexually. When she did join me in bed, I felt she wasn't really into it but just humoring me. That was frustrating."

"Did she suspect that you were looking elsewhere?"

"I can't imagine that she didn't suspect something, but she once told me that she didn't dwell on the negatives. My job keeps me out of the office a lot, so she assumed that my time was spent on legitimate things. I had been having the affair for five months before she questioned anything unusual about my schedule."

"How would you hide it?"

"Lots of different ways. I'd tell her about a lunch appointment that never really happened. I'd come home a day early from a business trip and tell her I was in town. I'd invent people who had come into town to be entertained by the company. It's easy to think of alibis."

Instinctively, because God's law abides within each conscience, unfaithful spouses know they are wrong, but instead of responding to God's voice, they lie so they can continue in temporal pleasure. The tragedy is that the deceptions only postpone the revelation of truth, and when it is exposed it is far more painful to everyone involved.

I received a letter from Tom's wife, Ellen, before he ever came in for counseling. It revealed that she had suspected his behavior more than he realized. It also illustrated the pain a spouse endures during such a time.

> Tom has never been one to share his feelings, so it wasn't unusual for me to be shut out of his life. But about a year ago he began acting unusual. He travels some with his work, but he always seemed eager to get home and relax. But what used to be two-day trips became three. And instead of coming home Fridays, he wouldn't make it in until Saturday. I had always suspected that he was a little too friendly with a female coworker because he constantly brought her name up in casual conversation. After nosing around I learned that she accompanied him on a few of his trips. When I confronted him, he laughed and made fun of my paranoia.
>
> On many occasions when he was in town, he said he was working late hours, but he came home smelling like smoke and alcohol. I suspected that he had been taking this same woman to bars, but again he accused me of looking for trouble. Our sex life took a nose dive, but he just attributed it to his weariness and my whining. I could never get him to talk about our marriage, in fact it got to where he would walk out of the room if I brought up the subject.
>
> Dr. Carter, I feel as if I don't know this man. He used to be a fun-loving man. We rarely ever fought, but now we're constantly distant from each other. I know that something is going on, and I'm pretty sure he is having an affair. Am I wrong to think this? How can I get him to open up? What's going to happen to our marriage if we don't get this resolved?

Ellen's lament is very common. In fact, it was no surprise when she called me a month later with the news that Tom had been "caught red-handed" with the female coworker. He said that he had been living a lie to keep from hurting his family, which showed his continuing commitment to deception. He may have wanted to keep his family from feeling hurt, but his greater motivation was self-gratification.

In order to reconcile a marriage ravaged by adultery, the unfaithful spouse must stop deceiving other people and the injured spouse should be able to cue in on the telltale signs of deception. If the unfaithful spouse comes in for counseling I work through these eleven typical deceptions so he or she can admit the deception and begin to work toward truth. Even when I counsel the faithful spouse, I still talk about these deceptions so that he or she will understand the pattern of lies controlling the unfaithful spouse.

DECEPTION #1: PHYSICAL WITHDRAWAL

When a husband and wife are feeling compatible they enjoy being in the same room, going places together, touching one another. Such togetherness communicates mutual respect. When one partner feels drawn toward a person outside the marriage, the desire for togetherness wanes significantly. The attitudes that once acted as a relational glue are dislodged.

The withdrawal can be manifested in many ways. The most obvious is often a decrease in sexual activity, as in Tom and Ellen's case. There is not only disinterest, but a deliberate effort to avoid sexual contact. Bedtime hours may change. Mysterious ailments may appear. Weariness may be feigned. Spouses may sleep in separate rooms. The words may never be spoken, but the communication is loud and clear: "Let's forget sex."

Additionally, the unfaithful spouse spends increased time away from home. Work hours are extended. Errands are run. Chores are manufactured. . . . Anything to avoid contact. Unfaithful spouses often admit, "I do not like the end of the day because it requires time with my mate." Even when the husband and wife are at home together, there is usually little touching or cuddling. Time is spent in different sections of the house. Eye contact is avoided.

The unfaithful spouse assumes that by not talking about his or her private life it is possible to remain unknown, thus keeping the back door open for extramarital excursions. However, he or she is overlooking the fact that nonverbal behavior also communicates a person's deepest feelings and desires. The one who physically withdraws is shouting, "Something is very wrong with our marriage."

DECEPTION #2: REPRESSED EMOTIONS

The deception of repressed emotions is closely related to physical withdrawal. If adulterers are to maintain their lifestyle they must minimize their personal vulnerabilities. Emotional expressions are usually bottled and little real effort is made to share feelings because such sharing can expose too much. It is common for these persons to complain that past efforts to express emotions had gone unheeded.

One woman typified this quite well: "Early in our marriage I attempted to talk about my feelings, but I never felt like we got anywhere. Instead of being understood I was just invalidated.

"So I finally began saying that I was not bothered even when I felt rage inside. What is worse, I got to where I didn't even share positive emotions. I did not express feelings of love, but I also had a hard time laughing at home and never talked about the good things. I was almost completely isolated in my own world."

Once the repression of emotions occurs, individuals display passive-aggressive behavior: laziness, repeated failure to follow through on promised tasks, holding resentments while wearing a smile, and purposely avoiding work projects. These individuals show signs of protest with the least amount of vulnerability. Authentic communication is replaced by phoniness.

I once asked Tom, "You mentioned that you and Ellen

seemed to avoid talking with each other, but surely she tried to draw you in at some time. How would you handle this?"

"Well, she got so used to hearing me say 'I don't want to talk about it' that she really quit pressing me. When I was at home, I would just bury my head in the newspaper or stare at the TV. She got to the point that she would unload her feelings on her friends and leave me out of things."

Unfaithful spouses may be on target when stating that their home life did not allow for healthy exchanges of emotions. Often a system of unhealthy communication was perpetuated by the mate, creating a distasteful atmosphere. It must also be acknowledged that this does not excuse the irresponsible repression of emotions.

DECEPTION #3: OVERT LIES

There has never been a case of adultery in which a lie was not told. Like Tom, each person committing adultery is aware that being honest about one's behavior might require giving it up. Sexual play can be temporarily fun, so adulterers do what is necessary to keep it going.

The most common lies told during periods of adultery involve extra time at work:

- "I have to stay late, but don't bother calling because the secretaries will be gone."
- "Looks like I'll have to go in for some weekend work."
- "We have some bigwigs in town from the home office and I have to keep them entertained."
- "Once we got started on this project, time slipped away more quickly than I realized."

Money is often spent in pursuit of the affair, so stories can be concocted about unexplained losses: "Looks like we had a few extra expenses for the house this month." Explaining time away from home is also quite common. The woman who meets her boyfriend during the day may tell her husband, "I had lunch with Susie, and you know how long we talk when we get together." Lies are frequently told about personal attitudes: "You are so important to me that I could never even think about another person." Additionally, untrue words may be publicly spoken in order to present the correct image: "My wife is the greatest; every man should be as lucky as I am."

Unfaithful spouses have allowed sociopathic traits to infiltrate the personality prompting them to fit morality to momentary whims. These persons make up rules as each event comes along. As time progresses the conscience is seared, and guilt has less and less of a hold.

In some cases, sociopathic tendencies become so ingrained that deception becomes habitual. For example, Tom once told me that he invented stories at times when there was nothing to hide: "It just seems like once you get started you can't stop."

DECEPTION #4: PARTIAL TRUTHS

Closely related to explicit lying is telling partial truths. Many times the communication of partial truths is rooted in preexisting patterns of relating. It is common to hear an unfaithful spouse remember experiences in childhood which required selective memory or incidences during marriage when the spouse could not be trusted with full disclosure. A habit developed of telling others what they wanted to hear while repressing issues that aroused strong emotion.

For example, Tom told me that his girlfriend was not the type of person who would call him often on the phone. This made it seem as though they had limited access with each other away from work. Later I found out that their offices were so close to each other that they did not really need to use the phone. Other examples of partial truths include:

- A husband fends off his wife's suspicions: "Of course I think she is a nice girl, but does that mean we are doing anything illicit?"
- An unfaithful wife may tell her spouse, "The reason I'm sluggish is because I've felt depressed lately," when the depression is fed by her guilt about the affair.
- A man may tell a friend, "She was in a really down mood and needed someone to console her, so I've become a good friend to her," not admitting that they also exchanged messages of sexual interest.

In a joint session, Ellen confronted Tom about the partial truths he had told her. "I'm not so worried about what you do tell me," she said. "It's what you don't tell me that keeps me on edge."

"What are you talking about?"

"Remember when you told me that you had to spend a day taking inventory at the warehouse?"

"Of course, because that's exactly what I did!"

"Yeah, but you didn't tell me that you asked to be given that assignment because you knew that woman would be there."

Most unfaithful spouses presume that if they present an image of being a responsible person, they will be beyond suspicion of extramarital liaisons. This form of deception toward others is merely an extension of the deception of self.

DECEPTION #5: DENIAL

Denial is another dimension of overt lying. In many instances, a spouse or acquaintance discovers suggestive evidence of an affair, as Ellen did, and makes a confrontation. The unfaithful spouse knows that it is their word against another's, so the deed is denied until the bitter end. The denial usually continues until the evidence is so strong that it forces an admission of guilt.

Tom's denial did not cease until a friend spied Tom in such an incriminating situation that he could no longer deny it. When Ellen asked why he had so adamantly told her falsehoods, he merely replied that it was part of the game.

When persons are committed to boldly denying any involvement in an affair, a spillover effect occurs. They not only deny the affair, but any emotion or activity related to it. Tom had previously told Ellen, "Not only would I never have an affair with Debbie, I don't even like her."

With this form of deception, wrongdoers become so committed to staying with the maladaptive behavior that an "I'll stick this out" attitude deepens. By denying sinful deeds and wishes they develop a hardness that becomes more ingrained as the behavior persists. There is a growing commitment to the deception and its behavior.

DECEPTION #6: UNACCOUNTABLE TIME

A major quality in successful marriages is mutual accountability. The husband who spends time out of town is more than willing to reveal his complete activities. The wife whose days are spent pursuing her own interests has no qualms about giving details about her day.

In an adulterous relationship spare time is "stolen" and must be covered up. One woman had every Friday off and had a large block of time with no family members present. If anyone asked how she spent the day, she would vaguely say, "Oh, you know how it is when you have a lot of errands to run." In fact, she had regular liaisons with her secret lover.

A salesman had much flexibility in his schedule and was frequently unavailable by phone. He used this opportunity to sneak time with other women, knowing that he could never be questioned about time away from the family.

Proverbs 9:13–18 describes a woman of folly who sits in the doorway calling to passersby to turn in for "bread eaten in secret." Those who turn in are naive says Solomon. They do not know that the woman's guests end up in the depths of hell. Time spent with no accountability to others will likely lead to personal ruin. Our sinful nature is so potentially strong that we need responsible relationships built on full disclosure.

DECEPTION #7: AVOIDING CONFRONTATIONS BY TAKING THE OFFENSE

In football the best defense is often a good offense. If a team can hold the ball for a long time, the opponent can't score. In human relationships the same philosophy is often used. Tom knew that if he was grilled with pointed questions, the truth might be found out, so he learned to use accusations and criticisms to keep himself off the hot seat. A familiar satire of the golden rule is applied: "Do unto others before they do unto you."

The first time Ellen learned about suspicious activities between her husband and another woman, she decided to talk with him calmly about it. When she began the conversation, Tom's eyes lit up and he snapped, "Wait just a minute. Before we talk about any faults I might have, let's have a look at the way you've been living the last few years." He launched into a tirade about many things he disliked about her. The scene was repeated later when Ellen again tried to ask questions about his outside relationships.

A wounded animal is the most vicious because it is in the most insecure position. If it feels threatened, it will attack quickly. The same can be said for a person with a wounded character. Deep inside the unfaithful spouse is insecure, knowing he or she has broken the rules. Feeling threatened, the unfaithful spouse will attack first and divert attention from his own misconduct. A common tactic to protect an insecure ego is to belittle another, hoping to elevate your own battered worth.

Mature spouses know that misunderstandings occur. To keep trust alive they speak directly about problems and desire openness.

DECEPTION #8: DENUNCIATION OF OTHERS WITH THE SAME PROBLEM

A woman asked how to handle the emotions related to her own divorce proceedings. She told me that her husband had been involved in a "one-time fling" with another woman, then confessed it. It seemed that he had repented, but a friend suggested that she make him pay for his sins by kicking him out of the house. Thinking this adviser to be a godly man, she followed his advice and filed divorce papers. She was unaware that this adviser had a history of sexual misconduct and was being severe in his judgment against the husband as a cover for his own past.

Individuals with unresolved sexual problems often assume a righteous public posture in order to give the appearance of being beyond reproach. *If I can create a reputation of being pure, no one will think of me in suspicious ways.*

Tom grinned sheepishly as Ellen recounted how he had reacted to the news of a local minister who had left the pulpit because of an affair. "For days you laughed and said that you would never trust ministers because they didn't practice what they preached."

"I know I said that. But it's true, they shouldn't be preaching if they can't live it."

"Tom, that's not the point! You said these things while you were in the middle of your own problem. Come on, you can't keep thinking that you are fooling me by pointing the finger elsewhere."

Most of these individuals grew up in a world that judged quickly and harshly. The people in their lives were so unrelenting in judgment, that they became afraid to honestly share their feelings. By joining the public denunciation of another who has erred, they keep a foot in both worlds.

DECEPTION #9: FEIGNING RIGHTEOUSNESS

Similar to the deception of condemning others is the person who carries a "list of good deeds" in his head, which can be (and is) frequently recited to others. This person reasons that a personal score sheet weighted with benevolent acts balances his misdeeds.

Church participation may be enthusiastically maintained. Efforts to get along with the children may increase. In-laws may be courted with new friendliness. Gifts may be given to the spouse for no apparent reason. Each of these behaviors can bolster the "nice guy" image and deflect the spouse's suspicion toward hidden sins.

Tom was not a deeply religious person, yet he agreed to serve on the financial committee at his church. "They needed someone who knew a lot about computers, and I was their guy," Tom told me.

"Did you ever feel out of place knowing that your personal life was not what you wanted it to be?"

"No, not really. If anything, it made me feel better about myself because I knew I was doing something worthwhile."

Tom used this good deed as "proof" that he was really a pretty good guy who didn't need to feel so badly about his adultery.

Persons living this deception eventually feel like hamsters running on an exercise wheel. Scripture clearly teaches that we cannot run away from our unrighteousness by enacting lawful deeds. Our sins must be rooted out by confession and faith in God, rather than in superficial activities.

DECEPTION #10: CHANGE IN DISPOSITION

Our lifestyles often reflect our moods. A person's peaceful, loving attitude often reflects a healthy lifestyle, just as an impatient, angry attitude suggests that something is awry.

Unless persons committing adultery are without conscience, they experience a change in personal deportment. At home and among close acquaintances they are usually more distant and evasive, more edgy and prone to criticize. They are often described as being in a fog because they are so hard to reach. Such qualities indicate something is going on "behind the scenes."

Upon being confronted these people may state, as Tom did, "I don't know why you have to pry into my business because there's nothing you need to know." Or perhaps they may vaguely explain, "Everyone has moments when they feel a little stress, and I guess I'm feeling a few pressures." Invariably their behavior communicates more than they are willing to state with words.

DECEPTION #11: BLUFFING TECHNIQUES

Bluffing skills are considered a plus in virtually any competitive activity. In athletics, the team stands a better chance of winning if the opponent can be confused. In many businesses the appearance of power and influence can be almost as important as the traits themselves.

An adulterous relationship automatically puts an individual in an adversarial, competitive position with friends and family, so bluffing is a commonly used ploy. It is most often employed when there is open suspicion of inappropriate deeds. When Ellen asked Tom to account for his time, he replied, "Oh, so you think I'm doing something I shouldn't do. Well, I'll be glad to give you a detailed schedule each day so you can see for yourself how I live."

Or perhaps a powerful statement of loyalty is offered: "You know how important my family is to me, so surely you wouldn't suggest I am capable of turning my back on the ones I love." The bluffing statements make the suspicious person's feelings seem absurd.

The bluffs are not likely to work if a person already has a reputation as being shifty or irresponsible. But if one is known as reliable, the bluffs will probably go unchallenged.

The list of deceptions could go on and on. They prove that the deceiver really does know the difference between right and wrong but is afraid to face the truth squarely. In fact, the unfaithful spouse is afraid to face himself or herself squarely. This deception is considered in the next chapter.

9

The Deception of Self

I had the distinct impression that Theresa was communicating conflicting messages as we spoke about her repeated problems with sexual misbehavior. She seemed to express a sincere desire to understand her behavior in order to make some adjustments. But a qualifier, which allowed her to feel less responsible for who she had become, followed each admission of wrong.

Theresa was in her early fifties and admitted that she was resentful at the prospect of growing old. She had lost her stylish figure about ten years ago, but men still found her quite attractive because she was cordial and self-sacrificing. After her two daughters had left home she reentered the world of work and discovered a much freer sexual atmosphere than what existed twenty-four years earlier.

"I really liked the looser ways," she explained. "When I was younger, people had fun but they were less open. I think it's time we had an emancipation from the old stodginess."

She had started an affair with a customer several years her junior. I was the only one who knew about this relationship, and she reasoned that she should halt the affair before her family discovered it. In spite of her conviction of its illicit nature, she had mixed emotions about giving up the affair. She told me, "I know this can't go on forever, yet I like the way he makes me feel. The affair is not right, but it has injected some excitement into my life."

When people like Theresa explain the facts of their extramarital affairs, it is not uncommon to hear the word *but*.

- "I realize that I should have thought more seriously about the consequences, *but* . . ."
- "I wouldn't want my own children to do the same, *but* . . ."
- "I was real lonely, and I know that shouldn't be an excuse, *but* . . ."
- "He wasn't really good for me, and I knew it, *but* . . ."

This three-letter word may go unnoticed by the speaker, however it communicates much to the counselor. *But* often suggests that I disregard the words just spoken and give more credibility to the words to follow. I usually find that *but* allows the speaker to minimize personal responsibility.

Theresa could look back on her life and see several factors that contributed to her tension. Her parents divorced when she was eight years old. She saw her dad frequently, but he was not very affectionate, and their attachment was not strong. Theresa's mother was kind but also weak. She was not at all assertive and did little to help ease the harshness of Theresa's military-like stepfather. In addition, Theresa was not popular with other kids her age. I asked Theresa to describe her peer relationships.

"I was always taller than most of the guys so I didn't have

many dates, and you know how cruel boys can sometimes be. But I didn't let on that it hurt."

"What about your marriage? How have you and your husband gotten along?"

"Lennie's family background wasn't much better than mine, so neither of us was really prepared for marriage. We had a whirlwind romance and married three months after we met. We did not get off to a good start."

"What hindrances did you encounter?"

"Well, I got laid off from work right after we got married. Then I had to find something to do just to keep our bills paid. When our first daughter was born I still had to go back to work for another year. Our second daughter was sick off and on for her first five years. Our early years were a real strain; Lennie and I never really recovered."

"By that you mean that the relationship soured early and it was hard to get back on track?"

"Uh-huh. I think if our daughters had been easier to raise, we wouldn't have any problems right now. Our lives have been more struggle than pleasure."

I deeply believe that part of the cause of adultery (and therefore part of the healing process) involves delving into unresolved issues from the past. Theresa would have had a stronger sense of contentment had she experienced healthier relationships. But because adultery is so closely linked to a habit of deception, we must be very careful not to hide behind historical problems. Ultimately, each individual must assume full responsibility for his or her own behavior, regardless of past wounds. Failure to do so increases the possibility for repeat performances.

SELF-DECEPTION

Over one hundred years ago, Bishop Ryle wrote that people "try to cheat themselves into the belief that sin is not quite as sinful as God says it is, and that they are not as bad as they really are."[1]

His message still rings true. If sin can be explained away, then it can be seen as less deadly than it is. However, true healing requires a total admission of wrong. In counseling, unfaithful spouses (and their mates, since they must understand their spouse's motivations) need to identify their common statements of self-deception.

"This Is Just a Phase I'm Going Through."

Childhood is often thought of as being the developmental years, yet adulthood also has stages of growth. Each year brings the need for self-evaluation and problem-solving skills. For example, each adult must ultimately address such issues as developing intimacy while maintaining individuality, making career decisions while satisfying family demands, or learning to influence others while communicating fairly. These aspects of adult growth take time and concentration.

Theresa stated that her parents had been strict about movies and other teenage activities, so she sat on the sidelines as her peers had all the fun. Then she married Lennie and had to struggle to keep a job and raise her children.

"I really feel that I'm doing some of the experimentation that I was not allowed to do in my adolescence. I have outgrown some of my family's strict ways. Granted, I'm not sure where my life is headed, but I'll get through this phase I'm in."

Restrictions in the past and pressures (family needs or careers) in the present deny many persons a normal development. These individuals reach a breaking point and unconsciously declare, *I'm ready for some self-gratifying experiences.* Such thoughts lead to rebellion prompting the person to assume, "I must be going through some sort of phase."

The unfaithful spouse *is* going through a phase, but such vague generalities cloak the truth. Unhealthy situations do not excuse behavior that destroys trust and inhibits spiritual growth. Theresa could make adjustments in her life that would not compromise her personal integrity. She could satisfy desires to be less tied to restrictive living by going back to college (as she desired) or by sharing in some wholesome fun with her friends. Self-deception is minimized by recognizing that phases of growth can be pursued within responsible boundaries.

"I've Fallen in Love with Someone Else."

Another common explanation for adultery is that the individual grew to love someone else so strongly that the sexual urge could not be denied. Unfaithful spouses usually admit that adultery is wrong but excuse it because of the intense or pleasant emotions that induced the affair.

Such rationalizations lack logic. What if an office worker was so thrilled by the beauty of a spring morning, that he or she decided to leave the office to play in the park? A couple of these episodes would inevitably carry the price of a good job. We all are tempted to "go with the flow" of our emotions but are fully aware that life can take disastrous turns if we do not resist these feelings when a higher obligation is at stake.

The assumption that the adulterous relationship is founded in true love is another fallacy. Romantic feelings may be quite prominent in such relationships, but they do not represent mature love. Genuine love is anchored in the desire to offer God's best toward another person, instead of lies and manipulation. In his book, *Money, Sex, and Power,* Richard Foster put this in perspective when he stated, "The New Testament regards romantic love as such a minor factor in marriage that it does not even mention it. That does not mean that romantic love is without significance, but it must be brought into perspective with the larger considerations for marriage."[2] The "I've fallen in love with someone else" rationalization allows a person to ignore the responsibility to formulate healthy strategies for alleviating a difficult situation.

"Our Marriage Has Been Bad for a Long Time."

Robert came to the Minirth-Meier Clinic for the treatment of depression, but after a few sessions he admitted having an affair with a woman fifteen years his junior. Together we determined that his depression was fueled by years of pent-up anger toward his wife, compounded by the guilt he experienced over the affair. He then explained, "My wife and I have fought for years. She is an extreme perfectionist, and I am an easygoing guy. If she had been more loving, this would never have happened."

"I hear a lot of pain in your voice," I replied to show Robert that I understood his long-standing frustrations. "You've felt like you were willing to give the marriage all you had, but it didn't seem that your wife would reciprocate."

"If you asked anyone that knows both of us, they would tell you that I'm the approachable one. She has the emotions of an ice cube."

"Was it your diminished sense of loyalty that made you vulnerable to outside attractions?" I asked.

"My loyalty wasn't diminished. It was totally gone. Maybe you can understand why someone else was able to make me live so dangerously these last several months."

"Robert, I'm hearing you insinuate that this affair would not have occurred if Dorothy had been a better wife."

"Absolutely. I hated going home each night."

"So you're admitting that she was pushing the buttons that controlled your behavior. You couldn't help yourself."

"Not exactly. I guess I had something to do with my decisions."

"Just *something* to do with them?" I asked, unable to suppress a smile.

He smiled sheepishly back at me. "Okay, you caught me. Maybe she hasn't been the greatest wife, but no one forced me to go out of bounds. It was my choice, and I'll take responsibility."

A sour marriage can present a variety of temptations to husbands and wives. The Bible recognizes our interdependent natures by its many "one another" instructions. Yet Scripture also indicates that inner peace can be found in spite of difficult relationships. After experiencing many rejections and disappointments the apostle Paul was able to conclude: "I have learned in whatever state I am, to be content" (Phil. 4:11).

Peter also indicated that even if our circumstances are difficult, we are not excused to live improperly. "For it is better, if it is the will of God, to suffer for doing good than for doing evil" (1 Pet. 3:17).

Individuals who claim that an affair was the result of a poor marriage would be more accurate to state, "I have had lusts and curiosities about the opposite sex. When my emotions prompted me, I decided to experiment with my secret cravings." Such a statement acknowledges infidelity as a personal choice, albeit under the influence of duress.

"If I Pass Up This Relationship, I Might Not Ever Find One As Good Again."

People do marry and then discover that their preferences or beliefs change through the years. This phenomenon commonly occurs in life. (For example, consider how much enthusiasm is lost after driving the same automobile for five years!) When the initial thrill is gone in a relationship, wishful thinking can become dominant, leading the individual to yearn for that ideal person who more closely matches one's dreams. When that person is found, a "this is it!" feeling occurs, and the individual bemoans the fact that the timing was too late.

Theresa, who blamed her adultery on strict upbringing, put it this way: "I was very immature when I married and really didn't know who I was. When I began finding myself, I realized I had married someone who was a bad match. I knew Lennie and I couldn't divorce, but I felt empty inside.

"Jack was everything I could possibly want in a man. We both wished we could have met under more legitimate circumstances, but decided that our personalities were so suited to each other that it was worth the risk to let the relationship grow. I didn't want to grow old without loving someone of my own kind."

"By putting so much emphasis on finding the ideal match, you are giving Jack a god's position. Do you realize that, Theresa?"

"You may be right, but I'm not sure that's all bad."

"My greatest concern is that Jack seems to be in charge of your happiness. If he loves you, you feel satisfied. If he rejects you, your world will come crumbling down. That's a pretty precarious position for you."

"But don't you agree that a human has to be loved? For years I've been yearning to have someone to know me inside and out."

Our modern obsession with "perfect love" is so overpowering that we feel cheated with anything less than the best. Armed with the false presumption that we can, or should, experience nothing but the finest, we justify immorality if it might bring personal pleasure. Theresa was deceiving herself with more than one rationalization. As she became attracted to Jack, she decided, "My marriage with Lennie has been bad for a long time," leading her to conclude, "It will never get any better." As her attraction to Jack increased, she told herself another lie, "If I pass up this relationship, I might not ever find another one as good." When she accepted Jack as a sexual partner, she rationalized her continuous involvement in the affair by saying, "This is just a phase I'm going through."

It was time to break this chain of rationalizations by helping Theresa see the real source of the unconditional love she was seeking.

"No human being can ever give you unconditional love, Theresa," I told her.

"I wish I could argue with you and tell you how wrong you are," Theresa sighed. "But I know that unconditional love comes only from God, not from humans. My recent experiences have really taught me how tentative human love can be."

"I have no argument with your desire for love. We all have that same desire. I know that living with faith in God is more abstract, but I also know that once you grasp it, you will have a far greater foundation for security."

At the same time that I was helping Theresa see her self-deceptions I was discussing these rationalizations with Lennie so he could join his wife in avoiding the future use of inappropriate thought processes.

"Stress Was Getting to Me and I Slipped."

When infidelity occurs it is easy to identify lifestyle stresses and blame the behavior on them. Yet we cannot be certain that our modern lifestyle is any more stressful than other periods of history. Mankind has contended with some kind of pressure ever since Adam and Eve hurriedly left Eden. However, we can argue that today's society puts undue emphasis on time and performance, which produces much tension.

Robert, the man who came to the clinic because he was so depressed, used stress as an excuse to rationalize his affair.

"I can appreciate the fact that your stress level has caused you to be more vulnerable to emotional ups and downs," I told him, "but let's examine the reasoning of this. If we all lay our problems at the feet of stress, then hardly anyone would be responsible for any wrongdoing."

Robert sat back in his chair and thought about my statement. Then he admitted, "I guess I've been burned out for a long time, and I've wanted to do something to register my frustration. The affair did that, all right. But you're right, there are other ways to handle my tensions."

"You recognize then that you may not be able to change the environment, but you can choose to take charge of your responses to it."

"Sure. I know other guys have wives who are not supportive, just as mine is not. In fact, others are in a lot worse shape than I am. But they don't have affairs. I've had a tendency to attribute all my troubles to family stress, my job tensions, and our financial burdens. Somehow it hurts less when I say 'stress did me in' than 'I chose my own problems.'"

Many people, like Robert, use the word *stress* as a broad catch-all to explain their problems. In doing so they overlook the real issues of internalized anger or poor time management. These must be identified before stress will be alleviated.

"I Don't Know Why I Did It."

Closely related to the notion of stress as the cause of adultery is the explanation: "It just happened." Presumably, some unknown something "out there" prompted the behavior. When people fall back on this explanation for immorality, they usually live nonreflective lives. Unwilling to explore what they really feel, they plod through life with a minimal amount of curiosity about what makes them tick. In addition, they frequently have a habit of defensiveness, prompting them to throw up a wall when personal issues need to be explored. They are communicating either "I don't want to admit why I did it" or "I don't want to learn why I did it." In both situations, those living behind the "I don't know" rationalization are being deceptive.

Everything we do is preceded by a specific choice. We do not always *seriously* deliberate over our choices (we often make automatic choices due to habit), but we always reflect about behaviors that involve morality.

There are many circumstances in which a man and woman get to know each other without consciously deciding to become sexually involved. For example, Theresa met Jack at her new job. At first they just talked casually. Later their conversations lasted fifteen or twenty minutes. Then they began eating lunch together. During the longer times together, they began talking on more intimate levels, which led them to decide to see each other away from work. Finally they decided to take their relationship as far as they could. Hindsight showed that while they did not start out intending the affair, it did not just happen.

At some point in any affair the decision is made to pursue sexual behavior. Whether blatant or subtle, the thought is nursed: *I want to go to bed with that person and I'm going to do it.* Whether this decision is made in a high moment of passion or not is irrelevant. The act is deliberate.

"I Deserve It."

The most self-serving rationalization for promiscuity is the one focusing strictly on personal rights. This is typified by the attitude, "Life has more than its share of difficulties, and they are supposed to be relieved by moments of pleasure."

I recall an unrepentant man who explained his extramarital

infidelities this way: "As a man I need sexual release at least every week, if not more. If my wife is not willing to cooperate with me, what else do you expect me to do?"

He seemed surprised and even offended when I suggested that sexuality is not a right but a gift, intended to communicate value to his wife. His subsequent "yes, buts" told me that he was not going to rescind his views any time soon.

Within the past generation, Americans have been swamped with rhetoric encouraging individuals to claim their rights. Some aspects of the personal rights movement have been fully legitimate because of the accumulation of abuses against minorities. But as is so common, the good becomes overshadowed by its excesses. Persons get so heavily focused on their own desires that accountability to others, especially their immediate families, is forgotten.

When Scripture addresses matters of marital relations, it rarely refers to personal rights. Even 1 Corinthians 7:4–5, which instructs husbands and wives not to withhold themselves sexually from one another except in times of prayer and fasting, emphasizes what spouses can give to one another rather than what they should rightfully receive. Throughout Scripture, God's servants are taught to set aside self-preoccupations in favor of a mind-set of humility. In doing so we imitate Jesus Christ.

Theresa winced as she admitted that she had succumbed to the temptation to let her rights take precedence over responsibilities. "Les, I'm not sure if you can understand how easy it is to get caught in the trap of feeling like you deserve something more than what you already have."

I assured her that although my needs had not driven me to the same results, I nonetheless could identify with her feelings.

"During my affair I repeatedly refused to consider Lennie's needs. I knew what I deserved and I wasn't going to be denied."

Theresa and I agreed that this acknowledgment was healthy since it could lead to an honest self-appraisal.

"This Just Isn't Me."

Joanne could hardly speak through her tears. A look of guilt and disgust enveloped her as she tried to make sense of the events of the last six months. She told me that until recently she had a wonderful life with a husband who was not perfect but certainly better than most. She loved her two children and wanted nothing more than to give them a good home. For years she had been involved in church activities and Bible studies. In spite of it all, she became sexually involved with a fellow church member. "I've been a Christian my entire adult life and never entertained the idea of having an affair. This just isn't me!"

When I hear this disclaimer my natural curiosity causes me to wonder, "Well, if this isn't you, who is it?" No one can jump inside another's body and say, "Excuse me, but I'd like to use your mind and body for a while. You sit over there until I give you back to yourself."

What these individuals mean is: "I have been forced to see a side of myself that I don't like, and I wish it didn't exist."

In one session Joanne seemed particularly distraught. I asked her why she was so upset and she replied, "Last Sunday an evangelist quoted the verse that says that the heart of man is more deceitful than all else and is desperately sick. Les, I always thought the Bible was a book of hope. I just can't stand to hear preachers talk about such negative subjects."

I responded gently realizing that the verse was forcing Joanne to question her rationalization. "Joanne, I'd like us to examine a paradox. Sometimes positive gains can be found by admitting our negative traits."

"But I feel so awful when I admit that I am capable of wicked deeds."

"It may not be a very flattering statement, but once you make that admission you feel a cleansing you never thought possible. It comes from seeking and receiving God's grace."

"Well, if God will forgive me after all I've been through it will be amazing. I know what I really deserve!"

"That's the point! Fully embracing your errors feels uncomfortable at first because you know the penalty you should receive. But when you receive God's forgiveness your feeling of joy far exceeds your expectations."

In His great Sermon on the Mount, Jesus explained that in spite of our attempts to look good on the outside we each have a propensity toward sinful cravings. He specifically called attention to sexual cravings.

"You have heard that it was said to those of old, 'You shall not commit adultery.' But I say to you that whoever looks at a woman to lust for her has already committed adultery with her in his heart" (Matt. 5:27–28).

Even if we have not outwardly engaged in adultery we are found guilty because of our inward tendency to desire illicit sexual excursions. It is part of human nature, emphasizing why we so desperately need the Savior.

An honest mind-set for the adulterer includes complete recognition that "it *is* me" who is capable of sexual sin. By admitting the depth of personal sin, the hope of restoration in Christ can be fully realized.

"I Was Seduced."

If previous generations could observe our cultural habits, they would walk about with bulging eyes. Some things would be welcome: attractive and colorful clothing, tasteful facial makeup, impressive landscaping and architecture. They would find the modern emphasis on physical beauty very appealing in many respects.

But other changes would horrify our ancestors. They would gawk at bikinis and see-through fabrics and watch TV and movie productions in disbelief as sexual situations are displayed with no sense of shame. And our hunger for the romance novels and gossip newspapers found in most grocery stores would perplex them.

Desensitized by familiarity, we are not fully aware of how our minds are weakened by such an overload of sensuality. We may not recognize how we respond to others in overtly sexual ways. Ultimately, this puts us in seductive situations.

Unfaithful spouses can indeed state that they have been bombarded with worldly seductions for years. When the right person emerges they are too vulnerable. They might tell of conversations so sexual that it was unmistakable that they were being pursued. They conclude that if the atmosphere had not been so seductive the sexual relationship would not have been consummated.

However, a choice was made to respond to the seductions. The Bible tells us to "flee temptations," yet we often *choose* to continue on. We seduce ourselves.

"God's Grace Will Cover Me."

Occasionally I talk with unfaithful spouses who have attended church for years. They quickly admit that their sexual sins are wrong, then add, "But the beauty of it is that God is gracious and understands better than anyone what I'm going through."

These people twist biblical truth to reinforce their thinking. God understands our thoughts better than we do; He knows what we will say before we speak; He knows when we will sit and when we will rise. He *is* acquainted with all our ways. He knows us as no one else does and paradoxically loves us anyway. The apostle Paul assures us that God loves us in spite of our sinful natures. God's justice would seem to demand that He deny us access, but His grace assures us that He will receive us—with no strings attached.

But there is a problem when we twist God's grace to excuse our wrongdoing. One man proudly told me, "Even though my affair is wrong, God's hand is in it, because I've been able to witness to my mistress and win her to the Lord." He told me that the affair continued long after her conversion, but with Bible studies. Then he gleamed with joy as he explained, "Sometimes we fail so God can prove His strength. God is showing me that He can use me for His glory in spite of my weaknesses."

The apostle Paul confronted such rationalization when he wrote, "Shall we continue in sin that grace may abound? Certainly not! How shall we who died to sin live any longer in it?" (Rom. 6:1–2).

Paul then reminded the Roman Christians that salvation includes a willful decision to consider the old self dead, in order to be committed to the new life in Christ. Grace continues to be extended even when we backslide into old ways, but we are not to belittle grace by stating, "Oh well, if I can't give up my sin, God will forgive me. No big deal." Sin hinders fellowship with God. Anyone assuming such an attitude toward grace is mocking God.

"This Is a Personal Matter."

It is easy to become so focused on ourselves that we forget how many lives are affected by our actions. This is particularly true when individuals are living in deception. Since adulterous behavior is usually known by such a small number of persons, the unfaithful spouse assumes, "What others don't know won't hurt them." Delusional thinking leads adulterers to conclude they won't be found out (in most cases they actually are), so little thought is given to how other people's lives will be adversely affected.

A single woman, who had been the mistress of a married man, told me that she was surprised at the number of people who were hurt by their relationship. "I assumed that his wife and children would be disappointed. But not his friends. They don't know what to say to him. And my friends have acted standoffish with me. Other family members and business associates don't act the same. Neither one of us can face the people in our home churches." Activities such as family gatherings and social functions weren't the same because so many people had changed their reactions toward her. She admitted that prior to the discovery of the affair, she naively thought of it as a private matter involving just her and her boyfriend.

Everything we do has interpersonal ramifications. Things done in private will affect our other relationships in some way. When we keep secrets, emotions are edgy and communication is guarded. Those behaviors are observed by others and our lives are wielding an influence. Life is not lived in a vacuum.

"I Was Under the Influence of Alcohol."

The use of alcohol is another common excuse for adultery. Often a man and woman will meet at a function that serves alcohol. The uninhibited atmosphere may cause them to say and do things. At other times they may drink an alcoholic beverage before engaging in sexual behavior—knowing liquor will "take the edge off" the anxiety of the moment.

Theresa told me about the first time she made sexual contact with Jack. "We were able to slip away from work early to a quaint lounge for drinks. It was the first time we had been any place together, except for lunches. You have to understand that when I drink a couple of glasses of wine, I'm much less inhibited. It put me in a vulnerable position, so when he asked me to

171

his apartment I just playfully went along. If we hadn't been drinking, I'm not sure it would have happened."

As is the case with many rationalizations, the influence of alcohol can affect a relationship. Alcohol *does* lower personal inhibitions and alter emotions and reasoning abilities. So it can indeed be considered a detrimental factor to the person committing adultery. It should be avoided. Yet the other part of the equation is that credit for personal behavior cannot be given completely to a substance. Alcohol can be a contributing factor to adultery, but it is never the full cause.

SELF-DECEPTION CAN CEASE

To promote a more honest self-appraisal, a commitment must be made to explore personal problems without excuses. Attempts to reconcile adultery with an "if" or a "but" tells me that the unfaithful spouse is not truly restored. There must be a willingness to state outright: "I specifically chose my behavior and I take full responsibility."

One client, Greg, returned to my office a year after a few weeks of unsuccessful counseling. "I've been involved with another woman in the last few months," he admitted at the beginning of our session. He said, "This affair will absolutely be the last one."

He seemed very different than when we had met before. When I asked why he could be believed he explained, "The last time this happened I knew I was wrong, but I became so busy telling my wife what she had done wrong that I didn't examine myself. Now I know that even if my wife leaves me, I have to take responsibility for what I've done, no blaming or rationalizing."

Three steps can lead toward the elimination of self-deception:

(1) A full confession with no qualifiers needs to be made. The unfaithful spouse should admit, "I did it and I'm willing to contemplate any problem that is a part of my behavior."

(2) Feedback from the spouse and from friends should be received without rebuttal. Even if confrontations from these persons seem incorrect, the unfaithful spouse will listen. This acknowledges our proneness to blind spots related to our own characteristics.

(3) A process of continued, open self-examination with a trusted friend or counselor should be accepted as crucial for personal restoration. Without such interaction we may be tempted to minimize the painful factors that need to be rooted out.

Infidelity represents a grave error in morality, but the mind-set and lifestyle of deception is even more serious. For true repentance, the unfaithful spouse must openly embrace the truth. The final step in counseling is to help counselees to examine their philosophies and to become committed to a way of life that is based on truth. We will do this in Part 4.

PART 4

The Process of Reconciliation

10

Sexual Fidelity
Restores Trust

"Look, let's be reasonable. Maybe you don't like the fact that I fooled around a little, and I guess I can understand your feelings. But don't be so old-fashioned. Having sex with someone else isn't the end of the world. It's not nearly as bad as you're making it out to be."

Michael was giving his wife, Janet, his very best sales pitch, but she wasn't buying it. Tears rolled down her face as she cried, "How could you be so insensitive? When we married you vowed that you would never forsake me for another, but now that means so little to you. I feel like I don't even know you. How can I possibly believe that you really love me?"

Was Michael's wife living in the Dark Ages with outmoded, petty, or unrealistic beliefs? If the modern scorning of puritan morality is accurate, perhaps he had a good point. Sexual excursions outside marriage might be considered an impish game, not moral decay. Yet if the Bible is still true and therefore trustworthy, Michael was flippantly winking at a deeply serious subject.

I believe the Bible to be God-inspired and thus without error; therefore I conclude that Michael's attitude was in need of repair. Sexuality is not to be entered into lightly or shrugged off with free-spirited notions. Christian principles of sexual fidelity within the marriage have deep spiritual roots. Contrary to humanistic ideology, sexual fidelity is not an archaic, arbitrary teaching passed on by rigid, judgmental prudes. Sexual behavior is intricately linked to the commitment of pure love God offered His human family. An understanding of the importance of sexual purity is found by thinking through the following series of questions about God's plan for our lives.

WHY WAS MARRIAGE INSTITUTED?

When Adam was given life, he had a perfect personality with a perfect ability to relate with God. He had a high sense of dignity since God had gifted him with dominion over all created things. Yet God knew that Adam would feel incomplete if he had no one of his own kind to love—Adam was created in God's image with a natural desire to receive and give away love. A wife was given for the purpose of more deeply experiencing godly love. As Adam and Eve shared human love, each became more appreciative of spiritual love with God.

Today, when a husband is kind to his wife, she is much more inclined to receive spiritual truth. When a wife supports her husband, he is more likely to be open to words from the Lord. Conversely, when there is tension or alienation, spiritual truth is more difficult to digest. From mankind's beginning, God's plan has called for marital harmony to be a conduit for spiritual wholeness.

This notion of marital love as a precursor for spiritual depth is captured in a brief phrase at the conclusion of 1 Peter 3:7. Peter had already instructed wives to be submissive, chaste, and respectful toward their husbands. And he had directed husbands to be understanding toward their wives, giving them a position of honor. Then he explained *why* they were to live in such a manner: "that your prayers may not be hindered." Peter was fully aware that if the relationship between a husband and wife is pure, so is the ability to commune with God. Marital love, above all other relationships, has the special designation to be an embodiment of spiritual love.

WHAT ROLE DOES SEX PLAY IN GODLY LOVE?

Adam and Eve sealed their commitment toward each other by becoming one flesh (Gen. 2:24). God ingeniously devised the sex act as a symbolic, intimate covenant with the mate, knowing that commitments gain depth when a sacred ritual is exercised. Sexuality is a husband and wife's "contract" which expresses the exclusivity of their love for one another, thus providing an experiential picture of God's exclusive love for His creation.

When Michael expressed his lighthearted ideas about sexual play, Janet questioned him, "Doesn't our marital commitment mean anything to you? When I married you, I determined that no one else would hold that position of honor in my life."

Later I talked privately with Janet and mentioned, "You really expressed some impassioned emotion regarding your feelings about sexual exclusivity. How did this affect Michael?"

"Well, I was pleased because that evening he told me that he had never really thought about sex as communicating so much. Morality was not taken seriously in his background. He had never been challenged to think deeply about the meaning of fidelity."

Many scoff at the idea of sex as a contract. However, it is

intriguing to observe the intense bonding that develops when two people have engaged in sexual intercourse. No one can deny that sex creates a hold, a knitting together of spirits, that cannot be logically or casually explained. Sexuality is the most powerful demonstration of commitment. For that reason possessiveness becomes part of the relationship once the line of sexuality has been crossed. This produces feelings of security and significance for marital partners, but for nonmarital partners it produces confusion.

Exclusive marital sex affirms the couple's commitment to God's ways and to the specialness of their relationship. A couple communicates to each other, "I honor you with a position held by no one else," and "I respect your need to feel significant." This enhances a mate's ability to discover dignity from the Lord.

One particular woman cried as she learned of her husband's love and sexual devotion to her. Her husband's best friend told her, "One evening at the gym the guys were discussing their various sexual conquests. Roger was real quiet, so they started needling him. They discovered his exclusive sexual interaction with only his wife and had some bellowing laughs at his expense." Determined not to succumb to their locker room crudeness, he remained quiet and went his way. As this friend related the incident, he noticed the wife's tears. Assuming her to be hurt, the friend asked if she was angry. Her response said it all, "I'm not angry at those men for being so rude. I'm crying because my husband loves me so much that he won't compromise his morals for anyone else!"

Why Does God Place Such Emphasis on Exclusive Sex Within Marital Bounds?

God is very insistent regarding fidelity for two major reasons. First, God is an intensely personal God who desires intensely personal commitments. He craves one-on-one relationships with each human. This is why Christ's teachings emphasize individual responses to God. Our Creator is not interested in seeing organizations, families, or countries come to Him. He relates to individuals. He has given every person a conscience which prompts him or her to assume personal responsibility to make an account to God. He has provided His Holy Spirit to stir the heart and mind of each individual, prompting each person to either affirm or deny a commitment to Him. This underscores the idea that His love is to be internalized rather than generic.

Even in the Old Testament days God instituted a ritual that demanded a very personal response to prepare lost mankind for Jesus Christ. When He chose Abraham and his descendants to represent Him to all the families of the earth, He required the males to commit themselves to God by giving one part of the body, the sex organ, to Him. The rite of circumcision served to represent an exceedingly personal contract with God. Abraham's nation was blessed because of this commitment to God.

Because marital love was designed to depict God's pure, complete love for each individual, He asks that we enter the same kind of personal commitment. When spouses reserve the sex act solely for each other, they demonstrate an understanding of God's intimate nature. The mandate for exclusive intimacy is neither petty nor arbitrary. Physical love, like spiritual love, is most complete when contained in a deeply personal and exclusive relationship.

The second major reason that God desires exclusivity in marital sexuality is related to mankind's deepest struggle resulting from the Fall. In essence, sin produced the overwhelming desire to have it all. Rather than desiring submission to God's scheme of right and wrong, each person is driven to indulge self's cravings. This trait was engendered in Adam and Eve when Satan enticed them to be as God. It is natural for each of their descendants to seek their own means of self-will, including sexual behaviors. God's requirement of sexual fidelity is one of many instructions intended to stem the tide of self-preoccupied living. This commandment can be construed as part of the process of being restored to Him, since restraint and self-denial cause us to become available to His indwelling presence.

Couldn't It Be Said That Sexual Exclusivity Limits Individuals in the Sharing of Love?

The rise of pop psychology in the last generation initiated an increasingly permissive view toward sexual love. Grounded in a humanistic philosophy, which believes that morality is not an absolute, many have concluded that sexual love can and should be freely shared. This thought was recently romanticized by the unlikely duo of Julio Iglesias and Willie Nelson who melodiously honored the many women who had been the objects of their sexual passions. "To all the girls I've loved before . . ." This philosophy presumes that sexual love, shared as broadly as possible, is the ultimate expression of personal wholeness.

Let's examine the implications of this notion. Sharing sex with multiple partners necessitates a brief commitment as compared to the lifetime commitment with an exclusive marital partner. Persons who jump from one partner to the next face each sexual interlude with an attitude that it will end whenever the thrill is gone. The security of each relationship is tentative—there is no guarantee of a commitment, only ultimate rejection. Love is based on performance, not on a mindset of giving. Sexual interplay is reduced to an external function that has little to do with a person's innermost spirit. Such activity is grounded in a "what's in it for me" motivation with little concern about the act's long-term effect on the other.

I asked Michael in a private session: "What did you think Janet's reaction would be once she found out about your sexual excursions?"

His answer told me that he either used much denial or was not at all contemplative: "Oh, I'm not real sure what I thought. I mean, I figured she would be mad, which is why I hid it from her. But I didn't really think she would be so distraught."

"In our last joint session she clearly expressed a feeling of rejection. It seemed pretty evident that exclusive sexuality means a great deal to her."

"Yeah, maybe I'm learning this too late. As soon as I went after another woman, she interpreted it as a rejection of her. I didn't think of it in that way, but I guess that's what my behavior implied."

"Let's be optimistic and turn this thought around. If she knows that you willingly put aside your temptations to become sexually involved with another woman, the feeling of rejection could diminish and your love would be heightened."

"Maybe so . . ." he nodded. I could see the wheels turning in Michael's head. He and Janet were going through their greatest crisis to date, but it was causing him to think about the outcome of his behavior as never before.

In the long-term, multiple sexual relations degrade human dignity. Sexual partners are reduced to objects of indulgence, and the person engaged in such behavior learns to live with a mind-set of usery and manipulation. Humans are made to relate to each other in the image of God, not by animal instinct.

RESPECTING GOD'S PLAN FOR SEXUALITY

If we understand that sexual fidelity within marriage is a sacred part of God's plan for mankind, several truths become clear. By embracing these ideas, restoration can occur.

Adultery Is Sin Against God.

I recently talked with a retired couple who was struggling with grief and pain because their son-in-law had left his wife and three children for another woman. They made a statement that is frequently expressed by people in their position: "We know that this is really an issue between our daughter and her husband, but it feels as if he has completely turned his back on us as well!"

Later I talked with the son-in-law, and he expressed that he had no idea that his wife's parents would feel so personally rejected. He also gave a commonly heard response: "I knew my wife would be hurt and that they would side with her, but I didn't really anticipate that they would see it as an issue between me and them." This man failed to realize that when he sinned against his wife, he also sinned against those who loved her.

God is the Creator and sustainer of each life and loves each person as His own child. When someone sins against one of His children, he or she sins against Him. Our heavenly Father deeply cares about the needs of each of His children. When we feel pleasure, He feels it with us. When we feel pain, He feels it too. No act goes without His notice and an emotional response from Him. He is intricately linked with humanity.

Unfaithful spouses, like Michael, expect God to be mad not hurt. Michael told me, "I felt a little guilty about my behavior after I had done it, but I never really thought about it as hurting God. I assumed He would be mad, so I tried to run from Christianity and my guilty emotions. I purposely overlooked my religious beliefs because they clouded the issue."

Once an unfaithful spouse admits that he has purposely grieved the Lord, I try to help him filter his attitudes and behaviors through an understanding of God's desire for his life.

"Michael, God is just. He holds absolute standards of right and wrong. But He is also loving. No law given by Him is primarily for the sake of making a person feel devalued. God loves Janet and wants you to be a conduit of His love for her. He has given you a wonderful role to play in her life."

"So if He feels disappointed with me because of my affair, it is caused by His love for her, not His dislike of me."

"God wants the highest for you too. He knows that if you follow His plans you will be a happier person."

Michael was capable of genuine change as he considered how his sin against Janet affected her relationship to God. It caused him to realize that restoration would occur when he would look beyond the behavior itself and face God who prescribed the ways of right and wrong.

An analogy: I may speed in my car because I am attempting to get around a slowpoke. But I may be apprehended by a policeman, a representative of the county and state because I violated laws created by the state, not the slow driver. I will then face a judge who will expect me to demonstrate a loyalty to the ones who make and enforce society's laws.

An unfaithful spouse may reject the spiritual significance of adultery, but his or her subconscious mind is aware of this truth. Paul told the Romans:

> For the wrath of God is revealed from heaven against all ungodliness and unrighteousness of men, who suppress the truth in unrighteousness, because what may be known of God is manifest in them, for God has shown it to them. For since the creation of the world His invisible attributes are clearly seen, being understood by the things that are made, even His eternal power and Godhead, so that they are without excuse (Rom. 1:18–20).

Innately, the adulterer knows that the sexual sin is not part of God's master plan, so the decision to act out is a specific rejection of that plan and of God who designed it.

Adultery Is an Act of Arrogance.

When an individual first seriously entertains the notion of committing adultery, an inner voice speaks a warning against such action. A mental struggle then ensues as that person weighs the moral reasons to refrain from sin against the personal craving to indulge in sensual desires. A decision to pursue the adulterous relationship means that the person has decided, "I'm above the rules that God has given mortals."

In a joint counseling session, Janet expressed her strong anger toward Michael. "How can you dare have the audacity to go out with that woman and then expect our family and friends to take us back into their circles! Don't you realize how high and mighty you've been acting?"

"Now, wait a minute. I may have a lot of flaws but high and mighty isn't one of them. You've got to admit that I conduct myself humbly most of the time." He then looked to me for reinforcement, hoping I would bail him out.

"Don't discount too quickly what Janet is saying. When we consider the subject of arrogance or pride, there may be some subtleties worth looking into."

For the most part, adulterers do not think of themselves as arrogant. Arrogance is open conceit or bragging, they reason. Since they have many moments of social appropriateness, they claim innocence of this trait. But another definition of arrogance is "blatant disregard for authority," which is not necessarily accompanied by loud clanging or pompous strutting. Instead the adulterer relegates God's ways to second-class status.

Adultery Always Has Consequences.

God gifted mankind with an innate desire for free will, but He also instituted a system of consequences as protection against unrestrained abuse of freedom. Consequences create feelings of guilt and frustration in the sinner which are part of God's plan to highlight the futility of sin and draw individuals back to His higher order of life. Solomon, the wisest man who ever lived, saw the benefit of such reproof. "Do not despise the chastening of the LORD, nor detest His correction," he said, "for whom the LORD loves He corrects, just as a father the son in whom he delights" (Prov. 3:11–12).

Consider the analogy of a broken leg. God allows pain so the person will be prompted to seek immediate attention. If God had not created a system of pain, He could be considered cruel, since greater damage would surely follow.

Similarly, to communicate His displeasure with sexual misdeeds, God allows the parties involved to experience a wide range of painful emotions. There will be struggles with guilt. Feelings of self-doubt and insecurity will abound. Formerly healthy relationships become strained. Communication with children and other family members is difficult. Life will not continue as normal because God does not want His loved ones to think of infidelity as a normal activity.

Some find it difficult to accept consequences that will be natural by-products of unfaithfulness. After giving up his girlfriend, Michael was angry when Janet still had difficulty trusting him. "Why is it so hard to convince my wife that our marriage will be fine? She doesn't seem willing to let bygones be bygones!"

Janet blurted out, "Michael, think about what happened! You completely violated my trust in you. I'm not going to stand idly by and let you assume that all can be normal."

"What price am I going to have to pay?"

"Well, for starters, I'm not going to just jump back into a sexual relationship with you until I can trust you."

"But Janet, that's not fair. Don't you think my confession is proof enough that I'm sorry?"

In our next session I tried to show Michael that Janet had every reason to feel hurt and angry. "You have to understand her hurt and anger and let those emotions run their course."

Michael had forgotten that any transgression carries consequences, and sometimes those consequences are powerful and long lasting. Rather than scorning them, Michael needed to remember Janet's negative reactions when he felt tempted to seek sexual pleasure outside marriage again.

For some, the consequences of infidelity spread beyond immediate families. Some lose jobs. Others forfeit church positions. Some live for years with a badly stained reputation. Others experience deteriorated relationships with children, in-laws, or former friends.

The fact that such consequences are so common indicates that sexual behavior is closely linked to a person's integrity and trustworthiness. It is not only the act of sex that causes others to have doubts about the unfaithful spouse, but also the fact that a vow was not honored and manipulation was used.

An Adultery-Torn Marriage Will Not Heal Quickly.

Common sense tells us that it takes longer for a patient to recover from open-heart surgery than from a tonsillectomy. The heart is more vital than the tonsils, therefore the body is much more intricately affected by tampering with it.

Likewise, sexual purity is so central to God's plan for our lives that when adultery is committed it takes time to heal. Often persons mistakenly push to get the problem of infidelity out of the way in an attempt to return to normal living. Doing so minimizes the seriousness of the act.

Michael and Janet had been separated for three months when Michael confessed to the adulterous affair. When Michael wanted to return home, I applauded his decision, then I suggested that they consider a step-by-step plan to help them ease back into full marital relations. However, Michael insisted on moving home immediately. Janet agreed, thinking that she should not risk alienating Michael further.

Within a few weeks Janet was back in my office, telling me how miserable she felt. She still believed that her husband wanted to work on their marriage, but it became painfully evident that he had not taken time to think through his emotions and guiding philosophies. They had attempted to patch the marriage too hurriedly.

I encourage couples to allow for a three- to six-month time period to "let the dust settle." For some couples this period may be shorter, for others, longer. Once painful emotions have eased, couples need another six months to establish healthier forms of relating to one another.

Only after Michael fully realized the extent of Janet's hurt did their marriage turn the corner. After much counseling he accepted that there would be some fallout from his affair. Janet was persistent in keeping emotional issues before him, so he developed patience and a new understanding of her needs. Janet and Michael remained under the same roof as they gradually witnessed a return of their love for each other. In retrospect they admitted that they should have reconciled at a much slower pace.

In a particularly uplifting session Janet told Michael, "One of the problems that led to your affair was your desire to have it all. Now I see your willingness to set aside your old tendency to be in control, and I am feeling more comfortable with you. I sense a real change in your attitude."

"Well, it wasn't easy for me to accept the slow approach toward reconciliation, but I finally decided that I would do whatever it took to prove that I'm different. If time is part of the equation, I'll give you all the time you need."

Adultery Requires a Spiritual Solution.

Whenever I counsel individuals who want to end an adulterous relationship, I suggest a number of lifestyle changes. For example, the other person needs to be considered off limits, with all contact coming to a complete halt. Accountability measures need to be put in place. New efforts to win back the spouse need to be implemented. Overloaded schedules need to be reduced to allow time for family matters. Communication styles need adjustment as do strategies for handling emotions. These solutions and many more need to be set firmly in place so the old lifestyle of deception can be replaced by a new lifestyle of wholesomeness.

These solutions will have little depth, though, if there is no effort to get one's life right spiritually. It is possible to implement all the externally correct behaviors and still remain vulnerable to the repetition of the old life of deception. All behavior is an extension of the unseen spiritual self—any restructuring that does not address the inner self is merely window dressing.

I talked privately with Michael, then with Janet, about their spiritual paths the past several years. Michael was quite candid when he said, "I've been taking advantage of God's grace. I was saved in college and had some real spiritual growth for several years. But then I let some bad habits creep into my life which I rationalized by saying that God would forgive me no matter what.

"I quit reading my Bible. I didn't really want other men to know of my salvation. Church was just a place to fill time on Sunday mornings. That was all a part of my demise. Now I'm committed to reestablishing my relationship with the Lord. I enjoy my daily devotional time. I hunger for the Bible instruction I receive at church. I truly want to talk openly about the Lord, both with Janet and with my friends."

Janet's thoughts were different. "My Christian habits haven't really changed. For years I've been consistent in my Bible study, daily devotions, and church participation. This whole incident has made me realize that I haven't been willing to let Michael share these with me. When he shunned his faith several years ago, I was too quick to write him off. My greatest adjustment will be to be more open with him about the Lord's presence in my life."

I suggested that this couple write out their spiritual goals, including the study, prayer, and church habits they discussed with me. Then I asked them to read those goals to one another as a commitment to meeting them. We prayed together and each of them committed to rely on God to give them the wisdom to be a conduit of His traits to each other.

Guilt is the emotion that prompts healthy spiritual introspection. Some humanistic thinkers suggest that guilt is outdated, but it is nonetheless a healthy emotion for anyone wishing to make amends for misdeeds. Healthy guilt is a true sense of remorse and shame, which leads to corrective changes in thought and deed. It prompts persons to compare the deficits created by sin with the gains created by virtuous living. And it acknowledges how the only true source of good is God Himself. When guilt is successfully worked through, people find peace in the lifestyle provisions prescribed by the Father who wants the best for His children.

Paul gives the Galatians a detailed distinction between the life that does not respond to the Holy Spirit's prompting and the life that does. The traits of the one who has not found spiritual depth include immorality, impurity, sensuality, disputes, and carousing. When God's voice is heard, the traits love, joy, peace, patience, and self-control become prominent (Gal. 5:16–23). A person who is not committed to the call of God will much more readily fall to the baser elements than the one fully committed to His ways. Without the Lord's guidance we have only human power and influence to guide us.

11

Truth in Marriage Maintains Trust

During the days of Roman rule the ancient city of Colosse was part of a prosperous tri-city network which included Laodicea and Hierapolis, just twelve miles down the Lycus River. The Lycus Valley was known for remarkably fertile volcanic soil. Large flocks of sheep grazed on the magnificent pastures, which enabled the area to be a center of the ancient world's wool and dye industry. The people of that region were among the few who had no need for funds from Rome for municipal projects. They enjoyed a wealth and life not commonly known in the mid-first century.

A few of the citizens of Colosse were Christians, perhaps the result of mission work emanating from the congregation in Ephesus. Colosse had a sizable contingent of Jews, but most believers were Gentiles who were not deeply grounded in an Old Testament perspective of the Messiah. They were vulnerable to the philosophies and fads of the day—particularly the heretical teachings that denied the total adequacy of Jesus

Christ and advocated a more tolerant view of sin. The prosperous citizens of Colosse had extra leisure time for a life of self-pleasure and its accompanying immorality. Within such a milieu, some Christians were inclined to believe that bodily sins were of little concern since the deeds of the flesh were presumably irrelevant to spiritual life.

Life in Colosse had given these new converts a long-time exposure to idol worship, which utilized sex as part of its ritual. Promiscuity was accepted with little opposition. So young Christians were already desensitized toward permissive ideologies.

The apostle Paul gave one of his most powerful instructions regarding immorality and its associated deception to the Christians at Colosse.

> Therefore put to death your members which are on the earth: fornication, uncleanness, passion, evil desire, and covetousness, which is idolatry. Because of these things the wrath of God is coming upon the sons of disobedience, in which you also once walked when you lived in them. But now you must also put off all these: anger, wrath, malice, blasphemy, filthy language out of your mouth. Do not lie to one another, since you have put off the old man with his deeds, and have put on the new man who is renewed in knowledge according to the image of Him who created him (Col. 3:5–10).

Paul desired that these Christians be *"renewed in knowledge"* rather than remain caught in the emotions and behaviors of deception. Truth was the only way to break the hold of immoral living.

Nineteen centuries have passed, but the parallels between the Colossians and modern Americans are obvious. We live in prosperity far beyond the world's norm. We take for granted luxuries that much of the world has never shared. We are particularly vulnerable to passions that feel good for the moment, even if they bring disaster over time. Regardless of the era, wealth and short-term, self-seeking pleasures have an uncanny way of co-mingling. So Paul's instruction to be renewed to true knowledge is equally relevant to us. Self-deception and manipulation can only lead to ruin. No one can juggle lies forever. At some point, truth has to be faced.

Some persons come to the counseling office ready to begin that process. One such person was Randy, a well-groomed man in his late twenties, trying to work his way up the ladder in corporate management. He had told my secretary that his marriage was shaky because of affairs discovered by his wife. During our first session, he stated, "My whole world has collapsed! I've been living pretty high on the hog for several years, and it's all catching up with me."

This was the first time he had ever been near a counseling office so I explained, "It would help me know you better if you could tell me about some of the circumstances that brought you to this point."

"Well, first you should know that I grew up with a solid church background. My dad was a deacon and a Sunday school teacher for as long as I can remember. My mother is also committed to the church. I've known Christian principles since I could talk."

"I understand that you've been involved in four or five affairs since you got married, so that tells me that you have put those principles to the test."

"Yeah. I've been running with a pretty fast crowd. I was married once before when I was nineteen. But that only lasted about two years. After that I decided to let loose. I'm not proud of it but I got tangled up with some cocaine users and tried some of it myself. I began drinking pretty heavily. When you're in that kind of atmosphere you have a pretty casual attitude toward sex. Marcia and I got married almost four years ago. She had been living a lot like me, but we've found that this free-wheeling lifestyle doesn't go too far in creating a secure relationship."

In the ensuing sessions, Randy and I worked hard to determine the underlying reasons for his promiscuity. We explored the subjects discussed earlier in this book. We uncovered his buried anger, his neediness, his habit of indulging in self-preoccupied thinking, and his rebellious craving for freedom. He demonstrated good insight and made progress due to his determination to live more appropriately. His wife, Marcia, joined him in counseling and discovered that she also needed to rethink her style of handling emotions and ways of responding to her personal needs.

As Randy's insights strengthened, we specifically focused on the subject of his deceptive behavior. He told me: "Les, I used to hide my real feelings when I was a boy because my parents punished me for thinking differently than they did. I learned that it was safer to *appear* to be compliant even when I had other plans. It created a pattern of dishonesty that got out of hand. I've got to get down to the basics and understand what it means to live truthfully. I know it sounds strange for a grown man to say this, but I'm not real sure what's true any more."

In order to break the deception of adultery, the unfaithful spouse must seek true knowledge, then *both* married partners need to become committed to truth as a way of life. Only then can personal healing occur and relationship be restored. When I counsel these people, I help them examine their philosophies of life so they can substitute truths for the lies they believe.

TRUTH #1: ETERNAL NEEDS ARE MORE IMPORTANT THAN TEMPORAL CRAVINGS

Every parent understands the vast difference between a young child's worldview and an adult's. Young children care little about economic trends, political elections, church and denominational ideologies, family feuds, or employment statistics. Their concerns focus on playtime, the latest toy or clothing fad, the weekend birthday party, and the assignments at school. Their lack of intellectual development creates a propensity toward simplistic, short-term worries.

In the same sense, adults have a difficult time comprehending the life beyond current time. We hear sermons and read books related to eternity, but we do not possess the maturity to fully process its wonders.

Yet it cannot be denied that each human has a spiritual, eternal quality that transcends the physical. No autopsy has ever revealed an organ that houses emotions or perceptions or ideas. These intangibles are manifestations of the spiritual self. To ignore our spiritual elements is to deny the essence of our lives. Therefore, the fully maturing person is careful to give the spiritual priority over the things that will one day cease to exist. As long as we hold a low view of eternity, we will be prone to short-term, pleasurable pursuits as Randy was. I asked him if he felt he had a good grasp of God's eternal plan.

"Les, I can quote you all the books of the Bible," he replied. "I can tell you just about any Bible story you want to know. I know my doctrinal beliefs. I've got religious knowledge coming out of my ears!"

"But that's not what I asked. You know many facts about the Bible, but I am wondering if your comprehension of eternity is very real."

"If you are asking how much I draw on these facts, the answer is, I don't. It's all rote memorization."

In the next weeks, Randy took upon himself the task of *truly* contemplating God. He read books describing God's character, His provisions for new life in heaven, His promise to guide each Christian by the Holy Spirit. He took time to meditate on these subjects. He prayed for God to assist him in keeping his spiritual thoughts at the forefront of his mind while he was at work and at home. He wanted Christianity to be real, not just memorized.

C. S. Lewis once wrote, "If you read history you will find that the Christians who did most for the present world were just those who thought of the next. . . . It is since Christians have largely ceased to think of the other world that they have become so ineffective."[1]

TRUTH #2: MUTUAL ACCOUNTABILITY IS PART OF A HEALTHY MARRIAGE

Several years ago I participated in a graduate students' survey to determine the traits most necessary for a healthy marriage. Over nine hundred professionals responded by identifying thirty-one traits they considered essential in marriage. Trust was at the top of the list. All others, they felt, hinged on this one. As I contemplated the significance of the survey results, it seemed to be an accurate assessment—every other aspect of marriage (sexuality, communication, financial management) presumes an element of trust. Furthermore, it seemed consistent with Scripture since God first asks us to trust Him, then we are given His promise of security and guidance.

One of the most difficult aspects of Randy's commitment to change was making himself trustworthy. I asked him to have meetings at least three times a week with Marcia so he could keep her informed of his various activities. He asked me, "Les, do you realize how unnatural this is for me? Ever since I was ten or eleven years old I have been guarded because I knew open disclosure would probably get me into trouble."

"You're assuming two things right now. First, you're assuming that you have some activities that must be covered up, and second, you're assuming that Marcia will respond as your parents did."

"Well, actually, both of those assumptions are wrong, particularly the first one. I'm tired of living two lives, and I'm determined to have no hidden agendas. I'm pretty sure Marcia will be okay in the way she responds because she wants things to be different almost as badly as I do."

Not only did Randy and Marcia share openly during their restoration period, but they came to genuinely enjoy their newfound depth of conversation. Randy learned that if he gave Marcia the chance, she would accept him, lumps and all. This increased his feelings of confidence, which in turn made him less likely to satisfy feelings of neediness illicitly.

No person should feel as though life is lived on a leash, but a bonded feeling is a necessary part of a healthy marriage. This is doubly true for the marriage touched by sexual sin. If questions are asked about "missing" time, the unfaithful spouse should be willing to give complete answers without being defensive. If outside relationships are threatening to the marriage, they should be curtailed. If extra measures need to be taken to make self known, they should be gladly enacted. Phone calls could be made during the working day. Schedules can be disclosed. Finances can be a matter of openness. If a deeper level of sharing makes the spouse feel more secure, sharing should increase.

No relationship is without some insecurity, but insecurities can be significantly minimized with a commitment to open sharing. The biblical writer James was interested in guiding his flock to wholesome lifestyle habits. In his epistle's summary statements he instructed, "Confess your trespasses to one another, and pray for one another, that you may be healed" (James 5:16). He was fully aware that forgiveness of sins is from God alone, but he knew that free accountability to others is essential to spiritual growth.

TRUTH #3: TRUE LOVE INVOLVES MORE THAN ENAMORED EMOTIONS

One middle-aged man did all he could to rationalize why he could no longer love his wife. "She's not the same person she was twenty years ago. She's heavier. Her skin is more wrinkled. Her hair is graying. She's not as energetic as she could be. I'm sorry, but the thrill is gone!"

I encouraged this man to carefully examine the implication of his words. If his love for her was contingent upon beauty-queen looks, it was going to be limited—the aging process catches up with all. Furthermore, what he called love was not really love but an enamored reaction toward physical beauty.

True love can involve feelings of elation, but deep marital love includes a feeling of "belongingness." The loving husband and wife know that no one else in the world knows them in the same intimate way.

As Randy and Marcia spent more time together, he realized how much he appreciated Marcia. "She knows all the simple things about me, like the way I like my breakfast, the shampoo I use, the clothing that I like best. I know these things are minor, but that's just the point! She knows me right down to the smallest details. I've realized how this represents a type of love that goes beyond romance. I have someone that I fit with."

As we each smiled, I replied, "It seems corny, but you're describing a type of love that most people overlook. By focusing on it, you find just as strong of a feeling of satisfaction as with enamored emotions."

"Yeah, it's like Marcia and I know all sorts of little secrets about each other that no one else knows. It gives our relationship distinction."

True love exists when partners learn each other's pluses and minuses. They know how to anticipate each other's moves and come to rely on the little things that distinguish their relationship from all others. The result is "belongingness," a familiarity that cannot be found in any other relationship.

This belongingness is accompanied by a feeling of pleasure and contentment which leads to spontaneous expressions of gratitude and appreciation. Sexual interactions are a natural outpouring of this form of love, though they may or may not always be highly impassioned.

TRUTH #4: SEXUAL TEMPTATIONS MAY NOT BE ELIMINATED BUT THEY CAN BE CONTROLLED

As Randy progressed in his personal growth he told me that he seemed to be handling his emotions and communications better, but he still struggled with sexual temptations. "I'm telling you, it seems that Satan knows my weakness because hardly a week goes by without the possibility of giving in sexually to someone I know. A lot of good-looking women are virtually begging for sexual involvement."

"You know, ten years from now I suspect you could tell me these very same words. The temptation will be there no matter how hard you try to avoid it."

"Well, it's a relief just to hear you say that it is normal to be tempted."

"The more pressing issue is what will you do when it happens?"

"Well, I'm already taking some steps in that direction. I'm committed to honesty and disclosure with Marcia, so that helps. Also, I stay away from people and places that will increase the temptation. Plus, I have a good Christian buddy that talks with me about keeping my actions in line with my beliefs. He says it's normal to be tempted, but it can also become normal to resist."

The apostle Paul described every man's struggle when he agonized, "For I know that in me . . . nothing good dwells" (Rom. 7:18). He even cried out as many do today, "Wretched man that I am!" His words strike at the heart of mankind's struggle with sin. We can desire to do right, but temptations from Satan can inhibit correct living. Once Paul admits this turmoil, he rhetorically asks, "Who will deliver me from this body of death? I thank God—through Jesus Christ our Lord!" (Rom. 7:24–25).

Paul's teaching was very direct. The power of God working in us is greater than the power of the tempter.

This truth has direct implications for those struggling with sexual temptations. Randy first determined to avoid circumstances that entice the flesh. This meant staying away from the parties he used to frequent and anchoring his social life with fellow Christians. Then, when he still found himself face-to-face with a tempting proposition, he chose to let God guide the moment. He would immediately breathe a prayer of commitment to let God have His way in that incident.

TRUTH #5: THERE IS NO SUCH THING AS THE IDEAL RELATIONSHIP

This truth is the opposite of the adulterer's rationalization, "If I pass up this relationship, I might not ever find one as good again." When adulterers explain the frustration and loneliness they have felt in their marriage, they often use the phrase: "I just wish . . ." In fact, the choice to seek after another sexual partner usually represents an idealistic pursuit of a person who will be closer to the perfect mold.

Many marriages are on wobbly legs before they get off the ground. This is caused by a family background that did not teach the couple to be fully grounded in truth, especially when that truth is ugly.

Young people are bombarded with messages that create lofty images of what a relationship can be, so much so that flaws are difficult to accept. Parents have few, if any, discussions with teenagers about a realistic approach toward love, with its many ups and *downs*. This leaves teens susceptible to impossible idealism. They may seem to have a broader understanding of love when they become adults, but they have little practice applying it. One woman told me, "Before I married I thought our relationship would resemble those toothpaste commercials where the couples just wanted to kiss and ogle at each other. Deep down I knew there was no such perfection in marriage, but I became very disillusioned when I found out how many problems we could have."

Our Lord explained that Christian values would not always produce interpersonal peace. Rather, Christians could expect moments of duress because they would automatically be at odds with worldly ways. Even when two Christians wed, strife still exists since worldliness and selfishness will not vanish from life until the day we enter heaven's gates.

Those who are working to avoid the deceptions of adultery need to acknowledge that each person is a sinner, meaning no person can be expected to perfectly fulfill the dreams of perpetual bliss. Satisfaction is a worthy desire, but perfection is unreasonable. These individuals must also admit that even if the current marital relationship is legitimately difficult, there is no ideal person out there who will permanently erase emotional pain. That role is reserved solely for the Lord.

TRUTH #6: MARRIAGE ALWAYS REQUIRES WORK

I often hear couples say: "I wish our relationship could be as happy as the Smiths'. They seem so suited for each other." Some marriages are more tailor-made than others, but no marriage merely falls into place without effort. Any happily married couple will say they have made a conscientious effort to respect the other's needs, attend to feelings and perceptions, and communicate with clarity and purpose.

Edward told me, "I have been dissatisfied with my wife for some time. I've only stayed married to her for the children's sake." Edward and his wife had completely different temperaments. Getting along for the past thirty years had been hard work. Both of them regretted that they were not as compatible as they had seemed during their courtship.

Edward met the other woman through civic activities and found their interests to be quite similar. After many engaging conversations, they became sexually involved and eventually discussed marrying each other. This woman's promise to Edward was appealing, "You will never have to worry about incompatibility again. My desires will be so consistent with yours that we will have little need to argue."

People in Edward's position find it hard to return to the original marital commitment because they feel like an exhausted marathon runner. They wish to retreat to a relationship of sheer ease. Yet they delude themselves. First, they wrongly assume that they have a right to a stress-free marriage. Second, they falsely assume that a good marriage can merely fall into place. Time and effort founded in obedience to God are necessary ingredients to marital success. If the work seems too much to bear, other solutions such as counseling and family conferences are more productive than an affair. Above all, a willingness to steadfastly work at the task of marital harmony is essential. This is consistent with Hebrews 6:10: "For God is not unjust to forget your work and labor of love which you have shown toward His name." When we diligently remain faithful to our Christian ways, we have the assurance that God will be pleased and reward us.

TRUTH #7: REAL CHARACTER IS REVEALED IN PRIVATE MOMENTS

Regardless of our intentions to be open, no one is completely transparent. Each person has some private windows left closed to even the most intimate of friends. Self-disclosure is impossible every moment of the day.

A person's character is truly revealed in moments of solitude. A person may seem to be a committed Christian, but spend little time alone with the Lord. Or an individual may show affection for the family in public, but rarely interact with family members at home. Public life can bring out the best in each of us since we tend to be image conscious. But the real person is the one revealed in the moments away from general view.

This truth forces unfaithful spouses to ponder the depth of their commitment to the Lord, the family, and wholesome personal habits. They can see in themselves what others cannot see. Accountability measures need to be established—to others, to God, and to self.

I talked to Randy at length about being more truthful in his relationships. Then we discussed how this could be made possible by having clean actions even when no one was near. "When your life is consistent publicly and privately, you can converse with your wife without worrying about guarding your flank."

"In the past I found it safest to say nothing. My private moments were spent doing things she wouldn't approve of. If I finished work early, I would go to a happy hour, then never breathe a word of it to her. Also, there were some shady characters that I did things with, and I knew she didn't like them, so I wouldn't tell her who I was with. I hate to admit it, but I began to buy pornography. It was then that I learned how to be really secretive."

"Now you're committed to truthfulness. So how will you handle these kinds of matters?"

"I could tell her about these activities, but that would break her heart. The best thing is to have nothing in my private life that can't be fully known. Besides, when I eliminate these hidden behaviors, *I'll* be convinced that my change is real."

Real character is revealed in private moments. Once a person begins looking truthfully at his or her actions, changes can be made that might not have been deemed necessary before. Quiet moments of reflective solitude can be accompanied by a process of mentally sifting through beliefs and feelings. Like the psalmist who agonized about his own morality, the individual can state, "Create in me a clean heart, O God, and renew a steadfast spirit within me" (Ps. 51:10).

WHERE TO GO FROM HERE

A major problem has been removed once unfaithful spouses learn to identify and admit the deceptions that have been a part of their lifestyle. Armed with truth they can make the necessary spiritual and relational repairs.

The next chapter examines ways to respond to one of the most common problems that lingers in the aftermath of an affair—forgiveness. Grounded by insights and by a commitment to truth, this issue can be resolved.

12

Forgiveness and Some Temporary Boundaries

Helen and Doug, the couple with two children mentioned in Chapter 2, had two different mind-sets regarding reconciliation. Doug's affair had been off and on for almost a year, but he felt they could readily put the past behind and get their marriage on firm footing without much fuss. Helen was not so sure. She wanted to take time, reasoning that she would feel more comfortable if they restored their relationship at a more methodical pace.

Impatient with her hesitance, Doug accused her, "You say you want to get things back to normal, but your actions don't back up your words. Your problem is a lack of forgiveness!"

"Doug, who said I haven't forgiven you? I've told you that I'll not hold this against you, and I still mean it!"

"Well, if that were true we wouldn't have to keep hashing things out. But you keep wanting to talk about our feelings, and you always want to discuss our family goals. You know that I'm not a great communicator, but you insist on putting me through this unnecessary regimen. I'm tired of being analyzed."

I could understand Doug's eagerness to forget their problems, but I was uncomfortable with two things: his resistance to open communication and his twisted understanding of the nature of forgiveness.

Turning toward him, I spoke, "Doug, am I understanding you to be saying that Helen's forgiveness would be demonstrated by no more questions or philosophical discussions?"

Shrugging his shoulders he said, "Well, we can only talk about it so much. She's got to prove she's forgiven me by letting go of the past."

"Doug, I know that it would be inappropriate for me to nag you for months about your affair," Helen interjected. "But you don't have to interpret me as being unforgiving just because I'm trying to discuss guidelines for our relationship. I don't think I'm being unreasonable. I still need hard evidence that things will be okay."

In the process of reconciling an affair, a delicate balance is required between offering forgiveness and the need to establish firm marital boundaries. Forgiveness is the pardoning of a fault while choosing not to hold resentments. It does not necessarily entail an immediate restoration of normal privileges and interactions. For example, if a teenager returns home late from an outing, he may be forgiven of the wrongdoing yet still be required to submit to future acts of accountability.

To restore harmony lost in an affair-torn marriage, couples can determine to respect each other's needs by openly discussing their plans for forgiveness.

HOW MUCH SHOULD WE TALK ABOUT OUR PROBLEMS?

Helen and Doug did not differ from most couples—she was more interested in discussing personal matters. Most marriages are typified by contrasting patterns of communications—one partner is more expressive than the other. Doug was more glib in social settings, but he was often annoyed when it came time to expose sensitive emotions.

Two extremes need to be avoided in the reconciliation process: evading discussions about the problems and discussing the problems obsessively. Evasiveness indicates a fear of vulnerability, accompanied by a need to dictate or control what will or will not be discussed. A delusion is also embraced as the evader assumes that the best way to remedy problems is to pretend they did not exist, in spite of the fact that problem resolution requires open admission and alternative seeking. If problems are not discussed, the issue of unfaithfulness temporarily may be set aside, but the home atmosphere which helped create the behavior is unlikely to change. I recall one man who declared himself cleansed of all problems a week after his adultery was discovered. He instructed his wife that any further talk about the problem would be counterproductive. In doing so, he ensured a continuation of an unhealthy home environment.

I suggested to Doug, "Helen's greatest need right now is to know deception is no longer controlling your behavior. And the only way she can determine this is to be permitted to peer inside your personal windows. This will require an adjustment from you."

"Does that mean I have to tell her what I've done during every hour of my day?"

Helen chimed in, "Honey, I'm not as interested in knowing what you *do* as I am in hearing about what makes you tick. And I want to hear how you feel about me. My goal is consistency in my forgiving spirit, and it can be accomplished as I become more aware of you."

When the problem is discussed too frequently (usually by the injured party), this also represents a type of unhealthy control.

The revelation of an affair leads to a feeling of being duped and completely out of control; therefore, there may be an extreme effort to compensate. In these instances the spouse is presented with an incessant barrage of inquiries:

- "How often did you see each other?"
- "Where did you meet?"
- "What was the other person like?"
- "What's wrong with me?"
- "How much money was spent with the other person?"
- "How am I going to ever believe you again?"
- "Do you realize the shame you've brought on us?"

These are legitimate concerns, but the questions may be repeated so frequently that an atmosphere of angry resistance can erupt. In such a circumstance, the questioner must honestly ask himself or herself if the inquiries are an attempt to induce extra guilt in the other person. I had to confront one woman who would not ease up on her extreme need to get answers from her husband. I told her that she did not seem to be absorbing the answers her husband was giving her; instead she was impatiently trying to make her husband responsible for her security. This was unrealistic and she was merely increasing her own anxiety and feeding her mate's frustrations.

SHOULD RECONCILIATION DISCUSSIONS BE STRUCTURED?

Successful reconciliation involves both the discussion of the problems and resumption of a casual lifestyle of daily routines. I usually suggest that couples set aside two or three specified times per week in the first few weeks for the purpose of sharing feelings, asking questions, and stating needs. By planning these sessions the goal is to avoid untimely ambushes when insecurity is at its peak.

I sensed that Helen and Doug were both capable of discussing their full range of feelings relatively soon after Doug's confession. We set the goal of having two sessions per week at home to talk about the history of their marriage and where they needed to change. These talks gave them ample time to explore each other's needs but were not so frequent that they did not have time to spend in more casual interchanges.

Two major rules are helpful for these discussions: (1) No accusing. The intent of these talks is insight. Accusations have the unhealthy aim of gaining superiority, which is a weak compensation for insecurity. (2) No defense. There is little true listening if mates are so busy defending themselves before each other. A competitive spirit grows as does the feeling of invalidation. There must be a commitment to truly hear the expressed needs and feelings of the mate. When this occurs so does the relational growth.

As an aid to these talks, it can be helpful to write out ideas and emotions beforehand so the discussions can proceed with purpose. For example, thoughts might be written about (1) areas of frequent conflict, (2) hidden emotions the mate should know about, (3) fears or concerns about the future, (4) the positive elements of the marriage which could be enhanced, (5) suggestions concerning ways to know each other better, (6) ways to make a more appealing sexual milieu. As these subjects and others are openly contemplated, the couple can proceed with a confidence in knowing that they are building on a foundation of openness and trust.

Doug and Helen found relief in their structured times of discussion. Doug had feared that Helen might begin to unload her feelings on him at unannounced times. Knowing that they would seriously attempt to stay within the agreed time frames made him less anxious about "communication overkill." Helen liked the structured approach since it insured that she would not have to coerce Doug into moments of interacting.

As the weeks progressed, these sessions became less frequent, from biweekly to weekly to once a month. They fully understood the need for sharing and reassuring to remain ongoing for years. They knew the seriousness of the marital commitment and that a broken union does not heal quickly.

WHAT MAKES FORGIVENESS SO UNNATURAL?

Whether an adulterous relationship dissolves a marriage or not, it is easy to harbor resentments for years. I have known men and women to be ruined emotionally because they could not resolve their grief with forgiveness toward the mate. One woman spoke bitterly about her former husband's womanizing which eventually ended their marriage. She recalled how he had made life difficult for her family by exposing their children to his mistresses and spending money so foolishly that they were seriously in debt. "I am still experiencing the repercussions of his adultery twenty years later," she said. "My children have developed their own rebellious behavior." Her greatest struggle was no longer with her former husband, it was with her decision to cling to resentment. Forgiveness would have required an unnatural effort, and she was too inclined toward her emotional reactions to allow her mind to override her subjective impulses.

God does not forgive us because we deserve it. He forgives us because it is His nature to love, and He chooses to forgive. Likewise, an injured spouse does not forgive because the adulterer ought to be let off the hook. Rather, this forgiveness is a manifestation of the commitment to live in God's love. This commitment is difficult because our emotional preference to maintain an edge over the wrongdoer can veto the decision to yield to God's nature. The injured mate may not feel very generous toward the unfaithful one, but he or she can choose to set aside the human instinct that causes grudges or wishes for another's downfall.

In my work with Helen, one underlying problem became abundantly clear. She had assumed messages of devaluation because she felt Doug's affair was a declaration that he deemed her to be inferior.

"Helen, the fact that you originally felt resentful over Doug's behavior tells me that you felt deeply hurt and betrayed."

"That's an understatement! He never showed me any respect. Then I started feeling very used. I did all the housework, ran his errands, and fixed his meals. But he never gave me a word of appreciation. Instead he was having fun with his mistress."

"In such an atmosphere you must have really struggled with feelings of lowliness."

"All the time. I wanted so badly to believe in my own worth, but when you get the message that you've been traded in for a new model, there's not much strength to build on."

"Helen, what are you trying to accomplish by holding on to your resentment?"

"I'm not real sure. I've never given that question much thought."

"Well, let's look at it closely then. When resentment stirs within, what sort of thoughts are you nursing?"

"Mostly I'm mad at him and I wish bad things for him. I know it's wrong to think that way, but that's the truth. I've suffered enough because of him, and I guess I'd like a little revenge."

"So you've been in the inferior position long enough, now you think it's his turn to be there."

"That's exactly right."

"Do you feel satisfied when you cling to resentful thoughts?"

"Maybe for a little while, but not really."

Helen readily admitted that lingering resentment was a futile attempt to compensate for the lowliness she felt. She had falsely assumed that she could exact justice if she could be convinced that she was really the better of the two. The resentment would easily return if her husband ever communicated an unwillingness to accept the inferior role. This is the most common reason individuals are unable to forgive.

When God chooses to forgive, the slate is wiped clean permanently. He remembers the sin no more. Unfortunately, no human is inclined to forgive as completely as He does. Our struggles with inferiority or insecurity prompt us to hold ourselves in superiority over the one who brought difficulty.

Two factors must be recognized to successfully forgive. First, we need to admit the coequality of each human. This is difficult for most of us since we see wide variances in each person's behavior. It seems strange for a moral, clean-living, gentle person to be deemed coequal to a manipulative or unwholesome person. Yet when we consider each person as coequal we acknowledge that each human has the same intense need for God's deliverance from sin. No person can claim righteousness on his own merit.

Second, since humans cannot forgive permanently, as God does, we must reaffirm our decision to forgive each time bitter feelings return. For example, when Helen told me she didn't trust her ability to forgive her husband forevermore, I replied, "I'm not as concerned about what you will do for the rest of your life as I am about the decisions you make today."

Our emotions do not always yield to our mind's logic and will return uninvited. Therefore, even when a decision has been made to set aside insecurity and forgive, a person can recognize the need to recommit to that original decision daily.

Forgiveness is a sign of successful grieving. It does not always evolve quickly, but the one who offers grace and mercy is eventually drawn into the qualities of the Father.

IS FORGIVENESS LOST WHEN FIRM BOUNDARIES ARE DRAWN?

Forgiveness is an act of pure grace, unmerited favor. If a performance is required before a personal debt is erased, it is no longer forgiveness. Forgiveness is never bought or earned. It is simply offered as a gift.

Knowing this, some unfaithful spouses are confused and even annoyed when forgiveness is declared, yet stringent consequences are set in place. They interpret the guidelines as indicators of vengeance or spite.

Doug's major complaint was Helen's insistence to slowly build back to normalcy. He did not like the boundaries she required as external evidences of his internal change: complete financial disclosure, predictable work hours, verification of free time away from her, no more social contact with his party-loving friends. He told me, "I can't help feeling that she is still holding a grudge. These measures are proof of it."

"At this point, Doug, let's give Helen the benefit of the doubt," I suggested. "Her requests *do* have merit and are her way of handling anger positively."

"I never really thought of it as positive anger."

Recalling to Doug's mind an earlier session in which we discussed how his affair had been the result of his own unresolved anger, I elaborated. "It would be safe to say that she has not been fully conversant with you about her past frustrations. She's been inclined to hold in her assertiveness, and now she feels like this approach backfired. By setting boundaries she is eliminating the possibility for lingering aggravations. She's doing something constructive by addressing her legitimate needs."

We discussed how forgiveness is the process of mentally releasing residual anger. But releasing anger was only possible after Helen became satisfied that she had appropriately communicated her needs. Forgiveness is the letting go of unhealthy forms of resentment but not the dismissal of constructive assertiveness.

To be sure that boundaries are being drawn in a constructive fashion, several key factors should be observed:

- The boundaries are a reflection of reasonable, considerate lifestyle concerns. For example, they may address such out-of-bounds behaviors as unexplained late nights, over-attention to a member of the opposite sex, or time spent with less-than-desirable companions.
- The boundaries should be stated without communications of condescension or condemnation. It is possible to firmly speak convictions and be simultaneously respectful.
- The boundaries are not motivated by a "get even" desire, but by a genuine hope that trust can be permanently regained.
- The purpose of boundaries is not increased restriction, but a milieu of openness and truthfulness.

CAN FORGIVENESS OCCUR EVEN WHEN THE SPOUSE IS UNREPENTANT?

Forgiveness is most readily accomplished when the offending spouse is fully cooperative in restoration procedures. Most fair people willingly let go of resentments when a genuine communication of remorse is consistently expressed. Doug was impatient to get back into Helen's good graces, but she was able to fully forgive because he genuinely regretted his involvement with the other woman. She told me, "There was never really a doubt in my mind that I would forgive Doug. After all, he was willing to renew his commitment to God and to our wedding vows. I just needed more time than he did to let my emotions settle down."

Helen was fortunate to have a happy ending to her nightmare experience. But what about those cases that don't come to such a neat closing? Many affair-touched marriages end in the divorce courts. Then, years of frustrated family problems follow:

- Children are shuttled between two homes.
- Financial problems mount as the family budget is severely altered.
- A new way of life must be pursued in the singles world.
- Friendships with other couples are put on hold.

In addition, some wandering spouses return to the fold without a well-established feeling of remorse. The marriage may be salvaged, but the injured spouse does not move forward with a real sense of confidence that loyalty is genuinely in place.

Injured spouses with partially repentant partners face the dilemma of offering forgiveness when there is no external evidence compelling them to do so. In spite of such circumstances, forgiveness can still occur. A fully restored relationship does require the cooperation of both partners, but restored emotions are a spiritual matter between God and the individual.

Forgiveness can be understood as a matter of initiative rather

217

than the result of another's show of repentance. Biblical writings include several examples of Christ offering forgiveness when none was asked or when the behavior did not warrant it. Christ's motive was twofold: He was a living illustration of God's unconditional love, and He refused to be lowered to the life typified by self-serving emotions.

Injured spouses can choose to forgive in spite of a lack of repentance because they know that a lack of forgiveness brings unfruitful emotions. In fact, by holding resentments they are lowered to a level of living that is little better than the deception they deplore.

The decision to forgive has little to do with the partner's level of repentance. Rather it reflects a desire to let the characteristics of God be foremost in one's personality.

IS IT POSSIBLE TO FORGIVE TOO QUICKLY?

When a spouse commits adultery, it is *always* best to maintain a goal of forgiveness. The alternative, resentment, carries such a negative impact that it is never a healthy choice. Resentment means that a person is responding to sin with sin.

Yet deliberation must be used as a spouse offers forgiveness to the unfaithful mate. Forgiveness cannot be faked or forced. It is not necessarily an easy decision that can be evoked at a moment's notice. A person's goal may be forgiveness, yet it may take time to painstakingly sift through the options before making a lasting commitment to that choice.

In some cases injured spouses offer forgiveness so quickly that they invite disappointments of mammoth proportions. Hasty decisions to forgive can indicate an imbalanced dependency caused by a need to have the mate's approval. It can be an act of desperation rather than true forgiveness.

Liz spent several counseling sessions with me because her

husband, Mark, had moved into another woman's apartment. "I doubt that he'll ever come home," she told me. "He says he's going to get a divorce then marry her, and he always follows through with his word."

"As a precaution, let's discuss an approach to take if he indicates that he wants to come home to you. Reconciliation would occur in a planned manner rather than all at once," I suggested. "Sometimes unfaithful spouses are impulsive in making decisions, and I don't want you to experience any more heartache than is necessary."

"I appreciate your concern. It helps to realize that I could suggest a slow, structured reconciliation rather than letting him jump in and out of my life. But I'll be surprised if he ever shows an interest in our marriage again."

About two weeks passed and I received a phone call from Liz on a Monday morning. Her voice was cheery as she said, "Guess what? Mark and I are back together. It's a miracle! Last Saturday he talked with a friend who convinced him that he should get away from his mistress and return home. So Mark talked with me about it. He said he would come home immediately if I would forgive him. So I did. He moved back in yesterday."

"This is a very sudden turn of events," I said. "What discussions have you had regarding the problems that lay underneath the affair?"

"We haven't touched on any heavy subjects yet. I told him that he would have to see you for counseling, so I think he'll be coming to your office next week. He seems very sincere."

I never saw Mark the next week. In fact, on the following Sunday Liz called my answering service in a panic. When I spoke with her she was crying uncontrollably. She told me how Mark had started contacting his girlfriend after only three days at home. When Liz returned from church that morning his belongings were gone and she found a note stating that he had made his reconciliation decision in haste. He could be reached at his girlfriend's.

Liz's drama is an example of what can happen when a person is so eager to forgive that reasoned deliberation is set aside. What she referred to as forgiveness was a clinging, insecure need for his approval. She had not made a well-rehearsed, logical decision to offer pardon. Instead she let her emotional neediness lead her blindly into an impulsive, ill-advised choice. Fear rather than true forgiveness guided her plans.

A forgiving spouse can consider the following to help assure that forgiveness is not too quickly given:

- The decision to forgive is the result of much prayer and meditation.
- No feeling of coercion or manipulation accompanies the decision.
- Forgiveness is not a hurried response to a person's clever salesmanship.
- The decision to forgive does not preclude the possibility that reasonable boundaries can still be respected.
- Forgiveness is fueled by calm confidence rather than insecurity.

Forgiveness is not easy, nor is it a one-time decision that never again needs to be reiterated. But once it is determined in earnest it can be truly liberating.

The next chapter examines ways to minimize some of the lingering logistical matters that can surface after marital restoration is under way.

13

Lingering Issues

Restoring truth to a marriage can be a tedious process, yet with insight and persistence it can be done. But some couples discover that residual problems can linger even after the deception is removed and an honest pattern of relating is in place.

Gordon and Diane went through an eight-month ordeal of restoring trust to their relationship. Gordon had been sexually involved with one of Diane's longtime friends but had felt so burdened by the guilt that he confessed.

"When I told Diane about the affair I knew it would hurt her," he told me, "but I wanted her to learn about it from me rather than from some other source. I was unable to live with myself anymore, so I was determined to give up my lifestyle of lies. I figured that the best way to reestablish credibility was to be straightforward."

Diane gave me her story.

"I was devastated when Gordon first told me about the affair. I not only lost my husband, but one of my best friends. But as the weeks progressed I couldn't help but be impressed with his sincerity."

I asked them to describe how they experienced healing.

Gordon responded, "Well, I first had to come clean with God, then with myself, then with Diane. I wasn't altogether sure what caused my actions, so I sought Christian counseling, which really opened my eyes to my habit of storing up emotions like anger and loneliness."

Diane was enthusiastic as she added, "When he would come home after a counseling session he was really eager to share his insights with me. This was so unlike his former habit of being uncommunicative that at first I didn't know how to respond. But now I'm beginning to trust in him in a way that I never thought possible."

"That's encouraging," I responded (a counselor always enjoys hearing good news). "So what brings you to my office?"

"Well, Diane and I are concerned about the fact that my problem isn't going away like we wish it would. By that I mean the other woman is still in our lives. Her kids know ours, and she makes it clear that she doesn't think that our relationship is over. Even though Diane's trust in me is growing, she doesn't trust this other person at all. I've got to get away from this situation."

The problems of infidelity (struggles with the third party, family and friends, or the mate) rarely dissolve easily. During sessions with couples like Diane and Gordon, questions about common residual problems of an affair are realistically discussed.

WHAT IF THE THIRD PARTY KEEPS PERSISTING?

In many cases the unfaithful spouse has a true desire to put the past behind and move forward with the spouse while the third party is unconvinced that the relationship is over. This person continually attempts to rekindle the illicit behavior. When this occurs, the restored person has the problem of keeping the chosen course while not doing anything to further antagonize the third party (though this may not be entirely possible; sometimes assertiveness is not accepted). In the meantime the spouse develops continuing anxiety about the possibility of a repeat.

The best case scenario removes the illicit lover from the scene entirely. The energies expended toward rebuilding the marriage can then proceed with much less tension. But in some instances the third party cannot be totally avoided. For example, the two may work at the same place or live in the same community. Perhaps their children are involved in joint activities or they may associate with one another in the same social circles. It can be very difficult to avoid eye contact or some form of conversation in such circumstances. Yet every effort should be made to minimize these interactions.

If the third party refuses to break off the relationship, all possible measures to permanently diminish personal contact should be explored. For example, when the other person works closely with the spouse and a change in job status is feasible but not too detrimental to one's overall career, this option should be explored. If necessary, social habits should be rearranged to prevent contact. In some rare cases it may be helpful to move to a new town.

In addition, telephone contact should be avoided. If the other party chooses to call on the phone, there is no obligation to engage in conversation. Some individuals may think of this approach as rude, but it should be remembered that the adulterous relationship is so highly offensive to God that He wants us to have nothing to do with it. The apostle Paul did not tell Timothy just to make a good attempt to avoid wrong behavior but strongly advised him to "flee youthful lusts" (2 Tim. 2:22).

Run away from them with all vigor. If the other party refuses to cooperate, an attorney can initiate legal action to make such pestering illegal.

Gordon's former mistress could find simple excuses to call him, even if just to chat. She would usually call him at work, but a couple of times she called his home. When Diane heard of this, she hit the roof: "I know you're back with me now, but you *cannot* let that woman hang on. It gives her false hope!"

Gordon admitted that he had a hard time being firm with this woman since it represented a complete turnaround from the days he spent with her. "It seems hypocritical to be involved with her, then to be so abrupt." Yet we agreed that the success of his marriage was so important that he would rather risk offending the mistress than his wife.

"Gordon," I said to him, "Diane is right. Any continued contact with the other woman makes her feel like the door is still ajar. She needs to hear you refuse her calls in consistent and unmistakably firm terms. Besides, you are fortunate to have Diane still on your team, and she is unquestionably your higher priority."

Gordon agreed to avoid verbal contact with his former girlfriend if they ever happened to be at the same event. He refused to accept any of her calls, even though she would say they were an emergency. And he was willing to let Diane know each time she attempted to contact him.

Months had passed since their affair broke off, but Gordon realized that he would have to maintain his distance. One slip would cause his former girlfriend to think that he might be ready to renew their relationship.

WHAT HAPPENS IF A PREGNANCY RESULTS FROM THE AFFAIR?

People in adulterous relationships are naive if they believe pregnancies can always be prevented as long as precautions are taken. That simply is not the case. Birth-control devices may be largely successful in preventing pregnancy, but they are not completely foolproof. There are also instances when a pregnancy may happen "accidentally on purpose." I have heard women declare that if they could not have the man they wanted, at least they could have a living legacy of him.

Whatever the reason for the pregnancy, the question about the status of the child remains. First, it should be agreed that an abortion is a morally inappropriate solution. The child may be conceived in sin, but the mother and father must recognize that a wrong is not corrected by committing another wrong.

Some might argue with my position regarding the father's role in the illegitimate child's life, but I contend that it is best to waive all rights to the child, as in an adoption case, and let the mother rear the child. The chances for the mother's return to a normal life diminishes if the adulterous father insists upon being on the scene throughout the child's growing years without the benefit of marriage. In addition, if the father is linked to his mistress for years, the possibility for a restored marriage lessens. Financial assistance may be necessary, but visitation should not occur. (If she is already married, full adoption may be the best solution if her husband wishes to continue their relationship.) In most instances the mother is single and has a chance to marry and establish a normal, healthy home.

I have known men who maintained visitation rights with a child of adultery, but in each case it created confusion. The jilted wife was forced to share a husband with another family, which only caused tremendous anger and mistrust. The mother was allowed to maintain a relationship with her boyfriend, which only reinforced her rebellious desires, and the child never experienced the nature of a normal family. On top of it all, friends and family were perplexed as to the best response. The child should have a chance to live as normally as possible.

A parental arrangement grounded in adultery is not normal.

WHAT IS REASONABLE ACCOUNTABILITY?

The methods of accountability initiated by the couple during the recovery process should be clearly enumerated. The unfaithful spouse should make phone calls informing the other spouse of personal whereabouts. When large amounts of unexplained time occur, which can be normal in a variety of situations, the unfaithful spouse should make every effort to account for this time. For example, a salesman who was out of the office quite a bit shared his daily schedule with his wife so she would feel comfortable knowing his daily activities. Since money is usually handled in deceptive ways during an affair, measures to ensure full financial openness should also be enacted.

Gordon told me that he found security in the fact that he had promised to keep his whereabouts known. "It's not that I distrusted myself. But I just wanted Diane to know everything about my day. When she would indicate her belief in what I said, I felt reinforced. This helped our reconciliation. I plan to continue this type of openness indefinitely."

It should be underscored that the injured party should avoid the temptation to badger or constantly pin down the spouse.

WHEN SHOULD WE RETURN TO A SEXUAL RELATIONSHIP?

A common mistake occurs when marriage partners return to normal sexual interaction too quickly. This may happen because the injured party is too eager to be affirmed as desirable once again or because the unfaithful spouse impatiently wants to sweep away the unpleasantries of a relationship in limbo.

One woman told me that she immediately became sexually involved with her husband when he said his affair was over, but it was a mistake because her emotions were more fragile than she had realized. She learned that feelings of security needed to precede healthy sexual communication.

Before sexual intercourse returns to the marriage, the couple should spend time courting. A comfortable level of pleasant conversation should also be instated—this form of communication is essential to a healthy relationship. Also, touching of a nonsexual nature should be free, holding hands or sitting near each other should be natural. When this form of relating is intact, *then* the couple is ready for full sexual contact.

Reconciling couples often find it helpful to inaugurate their renewed commitment with a weekend getaway. This gives them maximum concentration on each other with minimal diversions. It also provides them with an environment other than the same old place where memories abound. The key to successfully reentering a marital sexual union is to be relaxed rather than frantic, patient rather than pushed.

Sexual relations should be considered completely off-limits in cases involving a continuation of adultery. Two explanations are given for this rule of thumb: (1) If the unfaithful partner knows the spouse will continue sexual involvements, it encourages an attitude of manipulation and usery. The "I-can-have-it-all" attitude grows; (2) The injured spouse is inviting deep hurt when he or she has renewed the sexual bond only to learn that the spouse has strayed again. This causes a loss of self-respect.

HOW LONG WILL IT TAKE FOR THE TRUST TO RETURN?

There is no set timetable for the reinstatement of trust. Trust will be determined by the adulterer's level of repentance and the injured partner's willingness to forgive. It's a team effort. I counseled with one man who had consistently shown evidence of repentance for an affair that had occurred ten years prior. But his wife would use it for ammunition whenever she became angry, indicating that she had not chosen to forgive. The result was a minimal level of trust. Likewise, I have consulted with mates who were very willing to forgive, yet trust did not develop because the other spouse showed little remorse.

I encourage couples to allow a six-month period for emotions to cool down. Emotions such as anger, insecurity, or skittishness may abound for a while. There may also be a tug-of-war among the mates regarding the need to be close versus the need to have distance. These matters should be accepted as a part of the confusion and grief, which naturally accompany such a jolt to a marriage. The major rule to follow is one of noncoercion.

The six-month period should not be considered magic. It is fair to assume that most couples can resolve major grievances within that time frame, but there may be periodic emotional relapses when a reminder of the problem appears or when insecurity is experienced. The couple need not panic in fear that all progress has been lost when these temporary setbacks occur. Rather, they can accept these times as reminders of their humanness and of the continuing need to appeal to God for the strength they do not naturally possess. I am usually leery of the couple who very quickly declares that the problems related to an affair are completely past and normalcy has been restored. This is frequently a sign of repressed feelings and superficiality.

I have heard many encouraging testimonies from couples who "stuck it out" long enough to let the healing work its full course. While they never applaud the fact that an adultery occurred, these people find pleasure in their ability to claim

2 Corinthians 12:9: "My grace is sufficient for you, for My strength is made perfect in weakness."

HOW DO WE HANDLE THE WITHDRAWAL OF OUR FRIENDS?

Gordon and Diane expressed frustration over the fact that some of their friends had changed in their responses to them. Gordon explained, "I knew that some of our friends felt angry with me, and I can understand why. They felt that if I would betray my wife's trust, I must be a real scoundrel. The problem I'm facing is that some of our friends and acquaintances still act standoffish. It's like I've been branded for life."

"Diane, how do people treat you now?" I asked.

"Well, it's been interesting. At first, I got a lot of support. Three or four of my closest friends were especially encouraging and patient enough to let me cry on their shoulders when I needed to. But once Gordon and I began getting back together, some of our friends didn't exactly know what to think. Many had assumed we would get a divorce. I know that some worried that I might be setting myself up for a big disappointment by reconciling. That's when I noticed some people either shying away or speaking in very superficial ways with me. They wanted to avoid the whole subject."

I'd seen friends react this way to a reconciling couple before. "Two things come to my mind that might explain some of this. First, most people like predictability and they like to feel that they have a handle on their circumstances. But a situation such as yours presents question marks which are uncomfortable. They retreat not knowing how to deal with the ambiguity surrounding your situation. Secondly, I'm sure most of your friends are having to resolve their emotions related to your ups and downs. They have also been saddled with feelings of disappointment and grief. These emotions don't go away quickly, so it has the effect of throwing the relationship into a tailspin."

We decided that Gordon and Diane could handle the withdrawal of their friends by taking the initiative in two ways:

(1) They would maintain a confidence in themselves, knowing that they were both drawing closer to God because of their crisis. This meant that they would not continue to be unnecessarily apologetic. Instead they would be content, knowing they had turned a bad situation into personal growth. Their confidence in themselves might eventually elicit a positive reaction from their friends.

(2) They needed to show others that their relationship had been restored. They would be under the microscope in the future. Friends would watch to see if their love remained constant or if there were signs of tension. An "all is well" message would be visible when other people saw them being pleasant and gracious with each other.

Patience is a key element in the healing process. As friends realize that problems are in the past and feel settled in their own emotions, most relationships will return to a pattern of normalcy.

WHAT CAN BE DONE TO REESTABLISH TIES WITH THE EXTENDED FAMILY?

A reconciling couple must also successfully respond to the wariness commonly held by the extended family. It is true that a person does not just marry a spouse, but it is a package deal that includes the in-laws.

In most infidelity cases a family member is one of the first to be told the news of the affair. The injured mate is almost always the one who reveals the situation since he or she needs support.

Appealing to family members at such a time has both pluses and minuses. Family members are the most likely to know the couple's extensive history, thereby enabling them to know the couple's unique struggles, but they are also likely to be strongly biased. This may help the injured mate feel especially uplifted during the trying days of uncertainty, but it can create problems once the restoration process begins.

Diane's mother was the first person notified when Gordon's affair was discovered. Diane explained, "I knew Mother would be very biased, seeing me as doing no wrong while viewing Gordon as the bad guy. She's been available for me for so long that I had to talk with her. She's my greatest ally."

Gordon had a look of concern on his face. "I can understand why Diane went directly to her mother when the news broke, but it doesn't make it any easier on me now. I'm showing Diane on a daily basis that I've turned my life around, but my in-laws don't have that same regular contact with me, so they're not very far along in the process of accepting me back into the family."

I asked, "Have they spoken harshly toward you or ignored you?"

"No," Gordon replied. "We've had about four or five contacts in the last few months, and we've talked frankly about my decision to get the marriage back together. We're getting to the point that 'The Subject' isn't talked about when we visit, but our communication is pretty strained."

Speaking to Diane, I asked, "How extensively have you talked with your parents about your reconciliation with Gordon?"

"Well, I've told them that Gordon and I still love each other and want to try to work things out. But beyond that they haven't asked any questions, and I haven't felt compelled to talk with them about it."

Family members usually follow the cues of their own kin. I usually encourage each spouse to speak directly with his or her own relatives about their plans. Clear explanations should be given regarding the healthy goals being pursued. Optimistic statements should reflect the confidence that they are proceeding as well as can be expected, given the difficulties just experienced. Most relatives will imitate the attitudes of the one seeking support and encouragement. These conversations need to be repeated since family members will watch for any signs of regression. Regular updates should be shared so family members feel assured that the healing is steadily progressing.

Diane turned to Gordon and said, "I think it would be fair for me to be more specific with my parents about our progress. They knew plenty of the bad details during my down times, so I should balance it with the good news during our upswing."

"Honey, if you would do that for me I'd be very appreciative," Gordon responded. "They'll only believe so much of what they see and hear from me. If they sense that you're becoming increasingly comfortable with me, I'll be more believable."

The previously unfaithful spouse should not be so eager to resume favored status that he or she tries to force family endorsement. Relatives struggle with the idea that they too have been jilted, just as the injured spouse felt used and deceived. Their feelings will settle more slowly since they will not have the spouse's advantage of monitoring the healing from an insider's frame of reference.

WHAT IF THERE IS A RELAPSE?

Unfortunately, it is not uncommon for an adulterous mate to return to the marriage, only to have second thoughts about reconciliation. This is particularly true when the adultery has been occurring for more than a few weeks. Usually emotions fluctuate wildly, which can cause them to supersede common sense.

When a relapse occurs, it is clear that the unfaithful spouse has not developed the depth of resolve required to make the marriage work. In most cases the unfaithful spouse is resistant to the idea of accountability and clings to the illusion that complete self-direction is desirable. In some instances the injured mate increases the problem by excessively berating the adulterer for his or her deceptive practices.

Diane told me of a friend whose husband had an affair and then repented but returned to the mistress several times. "I couldn't believe she was so inconsistent," Diane said.

"When her husband said their problems were over, she let him return home, but she scolded him almost every day. So he left home and went straight to the other woman. But when he wanted back into the fold she let him return immediately. This pattern was repeated two or three times."

Shaking my head, I commented, "That type of behavior only makes a bad situation worse."

"I really feel that by letting him come and go she was doing two things," Diane said. "First, she was putting her own emotions through the wringer, and second, she was enabling her husband to continue behavior she disliked."

"So I take it that you differ quite a bit from your friend."

"Absolutely. I told Gordon that if he wanted out I wasn't going to try to put him on a leash. But I also told him not to expect me to beg him to come back home. I wasn't gruff in the way I spoke, but he needed to hear me declare that he couldn't play with my emotions like a yo-yo."

If inconsistencies are allowed during reconciliation, they only create a lack of respect toward the injured mate. It is an act of responsibility for the injured mate to continue restoration *only as* fidelity is maintained.

Coercion should not be used to keep a mate corralled since the insecurity would be so overwhelming that the marriage will probably collapse any way. The expectation of completely avoiding the third party should be clearly established, but communicated in a manner that recognizes the mate's free will. Also, the faithful spouse should resolve to avoid sexual relations with the repeating adulterer until his or her illicit behaviors are completely finished.

The injured spouse must communicate self-respect in order to elicit respect from the straying party. During the time spent apart, each spouse should review the issues outlined in this book, focusing on his or her own spiritual wellness and willingness to be grounded in grace and obedience to God.

14

Ten Principles for a Healthy Marriage

Linda and James sat nervously in my office as they recounted the events surrounding his adultery. In his mid-forties, James maintained an athletic build and a deep tan indicating an obvious pride in his appearance. This stood out in sharp contrast to Linda whose hair was fully gray and whose skin showed early age lines. Her haggard look told me that the last few weeks of her life had been as stressful as any she had ever experienced.

Claiming to have lapsed into a state of rebellion that he now regretted, James pleaded with his wife to give him another chance. Linda cried, "But what guarantee can you give me that this won't happen again?"

James explained that he was truly sincere, yet he winced at her demand for a guarantee. "I know in my heart that my problem is laid to rest, but I am concerned that you are going to be so demanding that I will never be able to meet your standards."

Frustrated, Linda turned to me and asked, "Do you think it's unreasonable for me to ask for a guarantee?"

I agreed that she needed a full measure of confidence that she and her husband would be working in unison toward the goal of restoration, but I cautioned her by stating that she would need to be balanced in communicating strong principles while also allowing James the chance to prove his repentant spirit.

It is natural to want reassurances that an adultery-torn marriage will never face the same experience again. Any effort not accompanied by a powerful commitment is suspect. Vows need to be honored. Plans and beliefs should be clearly delineated. Many measures can be taken to create a strong husband-to-wife bond. Yet, even the best laid plan can fail, particularly in the aftermath of a relational tragedy. This is why a very calculated plan needs to be enacted.

Sin continues as an option even for those who lead relatively good lives. A person can make a commitment to let God guide one's life one day, only to revert to old ways on another day. One woman told me that she had promised many times to soften her overbearing ways, yet she cried in anguish as she admitted how often she went back on her good intentions.

I reminded her of a similar lament written by the apostle Paul: "For what I am doing, I do not understand. For what I will to do, that I do not practice; but what I hate, that I do" (Rom. 7:15). Human nature is such that problems still erupt even after healthy commitments are made.

In spite of our natural inclination toward sin we can still hope. It is possible to become so committed to spiritual growth that the problems of the past become quite remote. The key to such growth is becoming submissive to God's guidance every day—a concerted effort must be pursued each day with conscious deliberation.

Jesus said, "If anyone desires to come after Me, let him deny himself, and take up his cross *daily*" (Luke 9:23, italics added). Paul told the Corinthians that he died to self *daily* in order to remain consistent (1 Cor. 15:31). Paul praised the Berean church for their consistent witness, which was largely due to their commitment to search the Scriptures *daily* (Acts 17:11). Only a day-by-day effort can be successful in changing old maladaptive patterns into new habits.

A couple can create a home atmosphere that may not guarantee perfection, but if they decide to follow certain principles, such as the following ten, they will reduce chances for further damage to occur within the marriage.

1. SET ASIDE TIME TO SHARE PERSONAL ISSUES.

Couples can agree to set aside time to keep one another informed regarding their feelings, needs, and perceptions, in order to prevent the communication gap that often results in recurring infidelity. Some spouses may resist scheduling these times of sharing, but this may be a necessity for couples who seem too busy or preoccupied to keep up with each other. A week should not go by without getting together to discuss the events and concerns of their lives. If possible, each day should consist of moments when a husband and wife can talk about the highs and lows. If there are times of tension, which require a cooling off period, this should be allowed *as long as* the tension is not suppressed in hopes that it can be avoided.

James and Linda decided they had little to lose by sharing their feelings with each other. They had been very close to divorce but then decided that they owed it to themselves to give the marriage every effort. Their efforts would put them in no worse shape than they were already in.

They had several long sessions alone at home within a two-week period. Linda had many pointed questions to ask him about his spiritual condition, his family commitment, and his willingness to structure his schedule to be more favorable to their family. She told me, "I was very straightforward in what I said to James. I can't say it was pleasant but it felt good to get my feelings out in the open."

I turned to James and said, "I know you're not used to such close-range interaction. How did you respond?"

With a look of relief he said, "I had never thought that I was capable of sharing personal things with Linda. I thought she was either too fragile or too unwilling to hear my point of view. But we took the attitude that we didn't have much choice other than to be open, so I gave it a whirl."

Linda revealed that they talked about pet peeves that had bothered them for years. They shared goals for their relationship. They expressed preferences regarding matters with their grown son. They coached each other on simple things which could bring back the feeling of consideration. She said, "I told him that he could win a lot of points with me if he would just open the car door like he did when we were dating. And I would also appreciate a pleasant word when he walks in the back door each evening."

These discussions were different from earlier talks because they were trying to explain their needs without accusing or demanding. They maintained a desire to truly know what needed changing. As a result invalidations and rebuttals were minimal.

When couples choose to become open and vulnerable there are risks of feeling hurt or being judged. Yet when this openness is a mutual commitment, it can create a camaraderie, which can carry them through moments of difficulty. God's full intention is that husbands and wives befriend each other to the extent that they each feel secure in knowing they have an ally who is willing to share in a "give and take" communication process. This alliance can only form when honesty and sharing are a regular part of the relationship.

2. EXPEND MORE ENERGY IN HEARING THAN IN TELLING.

One husband told me, "When I have something to say to my wife, particularly if it is personal, she seems more intent on offering a suggestion or rebuttal than absorbing what I said." The result was a feeling of invalidation and disrespect. The longer this communication pattern remains, the greater the gulf between the spouses becomes.

When a mate expresses a feeling or perception, even if it is confrontive or unpleasant, it is best to avoid the temptation to rebut and instead genuinely receive it. Each spouse must exercise fairness and patience, recognizing that it is normal for two persons to have two entirely distinct perspectives on the same subject.

As an example, in one of our first sessions, Linda was told by James that he could hardly express an opinion without feeling "walked on" by her. He told her that she was very quick to criticize or insist upon her own way.

Linda responded, "That's not so and you know it. Whenever you speak I let you have whatever opinion you want, so don't sit there and falsely accuse me!"

At this point Linda turned to me for my response (no doubt, my backing). Smiling, I told her that her response had just proven him correct. She had invalidated his perception that she was an invalidator! James had expressed an opinion and she quickly set out to explain that he was not allowed to think that way. She, too, began to smile as she realized what she had done. For the first time she gained real insight into her communication habits.

A good listener must be willing to consider a point of view other than his or her own. It can be most productive to state: "Let me think further about what you said," or "You've just made a good point." Paradoxically, when there is an allowance for a divergence of perceptions there is increased harmony. When understanding occurs, the speaker feels accepted and the result is usually an increased willingness to be cooperative.

3. CONFRONT PROBLEMS BEFORE THEY HAVE A CHANCE TO GROW.

One of my least favorite chores at home is pulling weeds. But it is one of those jobs that cannot be avoided. Nonetheless, I still have a choice. I can choose to let the weeds grow, then spend an entire morning weeding the beds. Or I can choose to make frequent checks of the ground and pull them regularly (before they have a chance to develop deep roots and spread). The best choice is obvious: Pull the weeds regularly so I can avoid that day when they will be so widespread that I'll have to break my back with a long session of undesired yard work.

This situation is analogous to any marriage. In each marriage difficulties will occur (just as weeds will grow). Two imperfect people cannot become joined in a perfect relationship. Yet each couple has choices about their response to the problems that arise. They can choose to confront them regularly so the problems will not have a chance to become deeply rooted. Or they can choose to allow the problems to grow and fester until they become so entrenched that it will take a monumental effort to weed them out.

Some couples choose to confront their problems regularly, but in such a confrontational manner that their difficulties develop deep roots anyway. They need to recognize that a habit of overstating their problems with rambling monologues does nothing to resolve difficulties and determine instead to be succinct in speech, considerate in tone, and eager to learn.

James and Linda had been married for twenty-six years.

Linda had assumed that they shared a comfortable and compatible existence, yet James was quietly dissatisfied because he thought his wife to be excessively opinionated and hard to please. Rather than talking through their differences, James chose to hold in his feelings; he assumed Linda would not like what he had to say. He became increasingly vulnerable to other women's affections and eventually succumbed to his affair. During counseling, James and Linda realized that they had been remiss in sharing feelings with each other, so they agreed to follow Paul's advice in Ephesians 4:26: "Do not let the sun go down on your wrath."

After several weeks of counseling had passed, I asked James, "You've been so hesitant to share feelings with Linda in the past, how do you feel about your new pattern of relating?"

He shook his head as he responded, "Someone needed to teach me how to openly respond to problems twenty years ago. Then we wouldn't be in the mess we're in now."

"Do you find it awkward to talk to Linda about the things that are bothering you?"

"Well, actually I'm learning what common sense should have told me before. By addressing little problems or personal concerns as they arise, they don't turn into major rifts."

Linda added, "We've both agreed that it's okay to disagree, and that helps us feel comfortable in our discussions."

4. ACCOMPANY A COMPLAINT WITH CONSTRUCTIVE SUGGESTIONS.

Criticism should be used quite sparingly since it easily leads to an insinuation of rejection and condescension. It is rare for me to talk with a person about an unsatisfactory marriage without hearing that one of the partners is excessively critical, a poison that will spoil a potentially pleasant partnership.

From time to time spouses do have a legitimate need to point out flaws in the other's behaviors or attitudes. Couples should not look for these flaws, and in fact they should be willing to accept the failings of one another with the understanding that no one can be expected to perfectly fit the mold. Yet there are moments when spouses should be direct in pointing out flaws, but only after carefully establishing a reputation as an accepting and loving person.

Criticism serves no useful function if we simply state what is wrong and then expect the solution to be implicitly understood. Rather, a constructive suggestion should accompany the complaint since the purpose of healthy criticism is to promote a desirable change. If the complaint can be stated in positive rather than negative terms, it is all the better. Rather than telling a mate, "You were rude to speak so abruptly," it would be more constructive to state "When you feel upset tell me in gentler tones."

Sensitive timing is crucial to constructive criticism. If the criticism is offered just as soon as a working spouse enters the door, it is not likely to be well received. Or if a mate is in the midst of a problem with one of the children, it would probably be ill-advised to offer a suggestion. The spouse should be considerate in both words and timing even when troubles need quick discussion.

5. AVOID EFFORTS TO BE CONTROLLING.

Control can be manifested in many ways: bossiness, manipulation, intimidation, threatening, possessiveness, and stubbornness. Subtle communications of control include pouting, the silent treatment, evasiveness, procrastination, lying, and tuning out. Each of these behaviors satisfies self while simultaneously forcing the mate into one's preferred response. These behaviors are likely to increase the possibility for strife—no adult wants such twisted domination.

Al sought counseling because of his wife's affair, and he stated quite candidly, "If I were married to someone like me, I'd probably have an affair too."

"Why is that?"

"Man, I look back at the way I talked to her, and all I see is domination. I thought that being a leader meant telling her what to do, and that's exactly what I did. She had to clean the house a certain way. I scolded her if she spent money in a way different from me. I told her who she could or couldn't talk to on the phone. I criticized her style of parenting. I'm sure she felt like a nobody."

Al concluded, "I want my wife to be comfortable with me, and to feel secure in the knowledge that I accept her as she is. I'm going to make every effort to refrain from calling the shots in her life. I'll give her credit for being a fully mature adult capable of living responsibly without my dictates."

Al learned that he could let go of the attitude of control, while still feeling free to express legitimate needs or concerns. He learned that when he decreased his craving to be in control, his influence over his wife increased. She sensed his willingness to be cooperative; in return she reciprocated with a cooperative spirit. Nowhere in Scripture is there an instruction for one mate to control another. Instead we are to consider one another's needs as more important than our own. Rather than focusing on control, servitude is encouraged. This concept is equally valid for both men and women. Men are given the responsibility of headship over their wives, but it should be understood that this is not to be taken as a license for dictatorship. Rather, it is an invitation for men to take the lead in setting aside controlling mannerisms in favor of service.

When control tactics are set aside there is a noticeable absence of the game of one-upmanship. This game is fueled by the competitive need to out-argue or to out-smart the mate so a "victory" of sorts can be claimed. Al realized that it was senseless to win a competition with his wife and lose their marriage. He decided to think of their marriage as a partnership in which neither person controlled the other. The competitive one-upmanship was replaced by loving interaction.

6. STAY IN TOUCH WITH EACH OTHER'S WORLD.

In a large percentage of adulteries the straying spouse will rationalize that the marital relationship had grown stale because of no shared interests; therefore, it seemed preferable to find someone who could more easily relate. This is true not only of people who have found a third party in the workplace, but also of homebound wives who have found someone who cares about their personal interests. It is unfortunate that some spouses become so immersed in their personal business that a huge gap exists in the marriage.

Mates seeking to maintain a successful relationship will make a full effort to know the ins and outs of each other's lives. What we do is so intricately linked to who we are that such knowledge can make a major difference in the understanding of each other's feelings and goals. It can be extremely beneficial for spouses to become familiar with one another's area of employment, since so much of our time is spent working. Questions of curiosity can be asked and interesting activities of the day can be fully shared. A spouse cannot be expected to have the full range of understanding of the other's activities, but genuine support can be expressed. James told me that he felt affirmed each time Linda let him explain some of the finer details of his work as an engineer. Linda did not always grasp the technical jargon, but James felt that she genuinely cared how his days progressed.

This show of interest should not be confined to the world of employment. Most individuals have favorite activities or family responsibilities which occupy spare time: reading preferences, outdoor activities, community affairs, extended family concerns, or local church pursuits. Spouses desiring marital cohesiveness will make it their task to remain informed about these areas of interest. In some cases this includes shared involvement and in other cases it means statements of encouragement. James often complained to me that he had little to say to Linda, but he later admitted that he had suffered from marital laziness. Once he made the effort to show an interest in Linda's many interests, James found they had many opportunities for warm conversations which led to increased cohesiveness.

7. MAINTAIN BALANCE IN TIME COMMITMENTS.

I have heard innumerable wives complain about their husbands' absences. Some husbands are so committed to work that family involvement seems to be an afterthought. Others can't wait to run away from the house to pursue extracurricular activities. Still others are at home so glued to the TV that they might as well be gone.

I have heard similar complaints from husbands. Some of them moan about their wives' excessive commitment to their employment. Others lament the wife's inability to say no to committee requests. Still others are overinvolved in the lives of their children.

A pastor friend of mine rightly concludes that the way to spell family love is T-I-M-E. It is not enough for spouses to state that they love each other and then expect love to grow with little real nurturing. Times of shared activities are necessary for communicating love and devotion. This time may be spent with family or friends, but it should also include moments shared with each other: periodic weekend dates, out-of-town excursions, evenings together in the den, or tag-alongs on Saturday's errands. When such time is spent together, couples are more spontaneous in sharing ideas or feelings.

James admitted that he had a bad habit of giving Linda the "brush-off" when she wanted him to spend time with her. If he had work to do on Saturday, he would ignore her request to schedule in some family time. Or if he went on a hunting trip, he made no effort to call her or to make up any lost time at home. When she wanted help in household chores he refused, stating, "That's not my job." During counseling James decided to spend time with his wife and family, even if it meant setting aside some of his favorite pastimes. He told me later, "I never realized how pleased my wife would be if I gave her some of my time. She shows such appreciation for our joint activities that I don't mind giving up some of my hunting and fishing trips." He also acknowledged that he would have been able to resist the affair had he made the effort to spend time with Linda throughout their years together.

8. KEEP RELATIONS WITH WHOLESOME FRIENDS.

There can be no doubting that we all are influenced by the company we keep. I like the straightforward words of Proverbs 13:20: "He who walks with wise men will be wise, but the companion of fools will be destroyed." Humans have an uncanny way of taking on the traits and attitudes of their closest associates. It's like learning a speaking accent. We do not intend to talk in a regional accent, yet when exposed to a dialect daily it is learned. Similarly, most of us do not intentionally set out to develop outlooks of immorality or laxity, but when we live with those who naturally manifest such attitudes, they rub off.

James and Linda told me that they had been forced to strongly scrutinize the influence of their social companions. They had befriended several couples in the neighborhood who were of the epicurean philosophy "Eat, drink, and be merry, for tomorrow you may die." So life had become one big party. Alcohol was a free and easy part of life. Sexuality was a subject that evoked laughter and lightheartedness. Spiritual values were placed on the back shelf since they did not fit this lifestyle. This hedonism could not be sustained without a cost. The exposure to this pleasurable philosophy led James to assume he could have his way with another woman without any harm to his marriage. During their reconciliation they realized that their neighbors had encouraged such waywardness. They discontinued these relationships.

I deeply believe that maturing couples need to join with others who have sound spiritual goals and habits. The apostle Paul suggests this to the Hebrews: "Let us consider one another in order to stir up love and good works, not forsaking the assembling of ourselves together, as is the manner of some, but exhorting one another" (Heb. 10:24–25). As a part of a body of believers who knows how to experience joy within the limits of wholesome values, a couple will find reinforcement for the values that will save rather than destroy marriage.

9. COMMENT ON THE ASPECTS OF MARRIAGE THAT ARE RIGHT.

Because all persons have insecurities (whether admitted or not), each of us has a need to be reminded that there is something likeable about ourselves. I have heard some disgruntled spouses complain that there is nothing to be liked in their mates. In most cases that is not true. While some do not display their positive traits as readily as others, there is almost always something good that can be stated. God created each of us in His own image, and while all have struggles with sin, each person has some imprint of His image. A mate's task can be to find what is good and cheerfully acknowledge it to the other.

Linda reluctantly admitted an attraction for men outside her marriage. Though she had been sexually active in her premarital years, she had refrained from the temptation to commit adultery once married. But it was a battle. However, James, sensing that he had only increased her vulnerability by being insensitive decided to play a new, nurturing role in her life. When we discussed the issue of praising Linda and noticing the positive elements of her personality, I sensed that we had touched a live wire. James sheepishly admitted that he could go months, perhaps longer, without so much as a thank you, to say nothing about a bona fide compliment. I asked him to consider an adjustment in this area. Several days later Linda talked with me and told me that she was unsure of the duration of James's commitment, but she was very happy because he had followed through on my suggestion. She commented, "I don't know how long he intends to say pleasant things, but I hope he doesn't quit. He has no idea how charged I get when he notices the good in me!"

Paying compliments communicates more than just a good scorecard. It says, "You're important. You are noticed. I like you. You have special things to offer. I am happy with you." Compliments become a glue that holds a relationship together even when areas of difficulty exist. Like a sports team that is comforted after a loss by the knowledge that they have had previous wins, a marriage can weather difficulties when there are sufficient memories of pleasant sentiments.

10. MAKE LOVE A MATTER OF INITIATIVE RATHER THAN REACTION.

In many respects each person is a reactor. You smile at me, I'll smile back. You act responsibly, I'll be responsive. You speak pleasantly, I'll want to respond similarly. God made us to be interdependent so we can be attuned to each other and responsive to personal traits. The reactive side of the personality is no accident. But it is a quality that must be carefully monitored since it can cause a well-intentioned person to be thrown off course by less-than-desirable circumstances. When one spouse is in a bad frame of mind it is all too easy for the mate to get pulled along.

A major element of a healthy relationship is each partner's realization that one's ability to love is not contingent upon the mate's behavior. The ability to be loving or kind or forgiving is contingent upon one's yieldedness to God. Love tied to performance is conditional, whereas love tied to commitment is a matter of personal decision. It is a choice.

We have discussed how deception and lack of insight are a part of the pattern of adultery. When we examine Scripture we find instructions to be open before God and to examine how sin can be set aside in favor of God's indwelling presence. Therefore, to inhibit the possibility of deceptive habits, each spouse must determine to make personal habits a matter of openness before God. An active prayer life is necessary to keep one's mind attuned to His will. Studying Scripture can create reminders of one's purpose in living. By being honest with God and committed to His direction, there is less likelihood that the spouse's weaknesses will create a misdirection in the other spouse's actions and attitudes.

Admittedly, it is easier to live for God when the spouse is doing the same. Yet, if this is not the case, it does not have to result in one's own spiritual ruin. In the healthiest of marriages each spouse will be willing to continue in spiritual growth, knowing that the partner might be positively affected. Ecclesiastes 4:9–10 offers a good encouragement for a shared commitment to live unto the Lord: "Two are better than one, because they have a good reward for their labor. For if they fall, one will lift up his companion."

SUMMARY

Eight months after James and Linda first stepped into my office, we had a particularly upbeat discussion. This day marked their last regularly scheduled counseling session. We each agreed that they would still have moments of imperfections, but we also felt confident that their efforts at self-improvement insured a strong probability of future successes.

I asked each to describe what they intended to do to maintain the momentum they were currently experiencing. Linda spoke first, "When this whole affair came out into the open, you'll recall that I was an emotional wreck. As I experienced the shock and grief, it became clear to me that I was more insecure than I ever wanted to admit. My anger, guilt, and fear were caused by the fact that I had built my emotional security around James.

"I know that I didn't always communicate in healthy ways, so it is no wonder that James wanted some relief. I'm determined to let go of my controlling ways. I also intend to maintain a reputation as an encourager rather than a critic."

"Linda, knowing that you have been willing to inspect yourself during a time that you could have gotten caught in the trap of just blaming James, I'm confident that this has been a productive time for you in spite of the pain," I responded.

James spoke up, "I guess I've had to face the fact that it's impossible to live without facing your emotions. I used to pride myself in containing my feelings, but I've learned that it only leads to bottled up anger and selfishness." Looking toward his wife he continued, "It may not be natural for me, but you can be assured that I'll keep an openness in my personal life. I've seen what it can do when I try to keep my personal life closed. It only causes deception."

This couple could expect many good days ahead because they had been willing to openly share their feelings and needs, to build new strategies of living upon an expanded understanding of each other, and to experiment with healthier forms of communicating.

Adultery is no minor problem to be resolved. Yet it does not have to lead to gloom and emptiness. When a mind chooses to become fixed on godly principles guided by Spirit-given insights, purity of living can be restored.

Notes

Chapter 1   You Are Not Alone

1. "Men, Fantasy and Infidelity," *Texas Monthly,* June 1986, 12.
2. Laurel Richardson, *The New Other Woman* (New York: The Free Press, 1985), 1.
3. Ibid., 1.
4. "Men, Fantasy and Infidelity," *Texas Monthly,* 12.
5. "Sex and the Married Woman," *Time,* 31 January 1983.
6. Jeffrey Weeks, *Sexuality and Its Discontents* (London: Routledge and Kegan Paul, 1985), 26.
7. R. J. Levin, "The Redbook Report on Premarital and Extramarital Sex," *Redbook,* October 1975, 38–44, 190–192.
8. William Novak, *The Great American Man Shortage* (New York: Rawson Associates, 1983), 24.
9. Josh McDowell and Dick Day, *Why Wait?* (San Bernardino: Here's Life Publishers, 1987), 21.
10. Philip Blumstein and Peter Schwartz, *American Couples* (New York: Morrow Publishers, 1983), 201.

Chapter 5   Excessive Neediness

1. Charles R. Swindoll, *Strengthening Your Grip* (Waco: Word Books, 1982), 160.

Chapter 6   Self-Preoccupation

1. E. M. Blaiklock, transl., *The Confessions of St. Augustine* (Nashville: Thomas Nelson, 1983), 281.
2. Ibid., 73.
3. Ibid., 261.

Chapter 9   The Deception of Self

1. J. C. Ryle, *Holiness* (Grand Rapids: Baker Book House, 1979), 10.
2. Richard J. Foster, *Money, Sex, and Power* (San Francisco: Harper and Row, 1985), 135.

Chapter 11   Truth in Marriage Maintains Trust

1. C. S. Lewis, *Mere Christianity* (New York: Macmillan, 1943), 113.